# ENVIRONMENTAL EDUCATION FOR SUSTAINABILITY

**FIRST EDITION**

## WILLIAM W. TOILI
*Masinde Muliro University of Science and Technology*

## EMMANUEL W. TOILI
*St Paul's University*

## MARY E. M. TOILI
*Vrije Universiteit Brussels*

Toili Educational Publishers

# Contents

# PREFACE

This is the first edition of the book that focuses on equipping the pre-service and the practising teachers of all subject areas with the current knowledge and skills in environmental education for sustainability. The book is a response to the demand for such a book by practising teachers, teacher trainees and trainers in teacher education at University and middle college levels.

The book targets students training to become teachers at the Diploma, undergraduate and postgraduate levels. The book will also be a useful resource material for practising teachers in all subjects in secondary schools and quality assurance officers and teacher trainers in universities and colleges. Those working with NGOs and other private and public organizations charged with the responsibility of creating environmental awareness and promoting sustainable development and education for sustainable development (ESD) activities will find this book necessary.

The book is based on the premise that while both potential and practising teachers are fairly well grounded in the various courses in their subject areas, they may be ill-equipped to satisfy the requirement that all teachers need to infuse environmental knowledge, skills, attitudes and values in their subject areas and align them to the ideals of sustainability. This makes it necessary for them to be exposed to the strategies for instruction in environmental education for sustainability, particularly when it is clear that students need to develop competencies required for sustainable living. The other personnel working with NGOs, public and private organisations concerned with ESD and promotion of sustainable development activities equally need such information and skills to be able to diligently discharge their duties. This book is about how we can help those under our care and guidance to prepare adequately for their contribution to sustainable living and sustainable future.

The book is presented in a simple, clear and Standard English language augmented with diagrammatic illustrations, pictures and tables that are intended to motivate the reader. The book has also several tasks and exercises to get the readers to reflect on what they read and to further extend their knowledge. In addition, the book provides a summary of the information at the end of each chapter to help the reader recapitulate the content of the chapter.

# FOREWORD

### Scope of the course

For many years since the United Nations Conference on the Human Environment held in Stockholm in 1972, environmental education has continued to develop knowledge about the environment and to propagate attitudes that help to establish an ethic of caring towards the natural world. In addition, it has attempted to recognise the need to engage communities in order to address the various environmental problems and issues. Despite the efforts in promoting environmental education through formal and informal settings, environmental degradation has continued throughout the world. This point to some weaknesses in the focus of environmental education.

Environmental education as we know it today has tended to focus more on safeguarding the natural environment or ecological dimension but ignoring in a germane manner the contribution of social, economic and political dimensions to environmental destruction. The pedagogical approaches used have been narrow in scope and failed to promote an understanding of the complexity of the world in which we live and the knowledge, critical thinking skills, values and capacity to participate in decision making about environmental and development issues. There is every need for schools and other institutions to prepare and empower learners to assume responsibility for creating and enjoying a sustainable future. We need a transformative education that benefits from creative and innovative teaching and learning. Sustainability is now more of a rule than an exception that should be promoted through environmental education. Environmental education for sustainability is currently a new approach to teaching and learning about the environment.

Environmental education for sustainability focuses on all components that impact on the environment, namely, social, ecological, economic, and political dimensions. This new look at environmental education is influenced by "Education for Sustainable Development" that is viewed as a life-wide and lifelong endeavour which challenges individuals, institutions and societies to view tomorrow as a day that belongs to all of us, or it will not belong to anyone (United Nations Decade for Sustainable Development 2005-2014).

As a potential educator, this book introduces you to the broad concept of environmental education. You will learn about the basic concepts of environmental education focusing on the need for sustainable living as espoused in the Earth Charter, Caring for the Earth and Sustainable Development Goals. It will introduce you to the nature of the environment, history of environmental education and its progress to environmental education for sustainability, environment, development, and sustainability, the curriculum in environmental education, strategies of teaching environmental education across the curriculum, and environmental conservation and management for sustainable development. It will give an opportunity to participate actively in environmental conservation and management in your local environment.

This book is divided into 14 chapters. Every chapter consists of several subtopics. You will be required to read and understand each chapter before you proceed to the next chapter. In every chapter you will come across important tasks like conducting an activity, collecting data in the community, or checking out on other related modules. At the end of every chapter, you will find a self-check directing you to assess your understanding and to give yourself a score in order to measure your level of achievement.

## Expected Learning Outcomes of the Course

By the end of the course you should be able to:

- Demonstrate an awareness of the role of the Earth's delicate balance of nature in the very survival of humankind and all other forms of life;
- Examine the contribution of environmental beliefs, attitudes and values by various societies on the present state of the Earth's environment;
- Demonstrate an understanding of the dynamics of sustainable development and its significance in promoting a sustainable future;
- Explain the role of environmental education for sustainability in fostering positive environmental conservation and management;
- Participate in protecting and improving the quality of their local environments; and
- Provide professional leadership in a variety of education settings both formal and informal, by developing, teaching, managing and evaluating environmental education programmes.

# ABOUT THE AUTHORS

**William W. Toili** is a professor of Science and Environmental Education at the Masinde Muliro University of Science and Technology, Kenya. He is a specialist in the study of Biology and Teacher Education. He is also a peer reviewer for the Commission for University Education (CUE) and a member of the Inter-University Council for East Africa (IUCEA). He has also published numerous articles in refereed journals (wtoili@yahoo.com).

**Emmanuel W. Toili** is an Adjunct Lecturer with St Paul's University, Kenya. He is also a PhD Researcher with the University of Nairobi, with interests in Agricultural Information and Communication Management. His focus is on enhancing the creation of an information management system that would promote efforts in harnessing biological systems to achieve food security, sustainable development and peacekeeping for all humanity. (emmanueltoili@gmail.com).

**Mary E. M. Toili** is a PhD Researcher in the Bioengineering Sciences Department at the Vrije Universiteit Brussels (VUB), Belgium. Her research interests revolve around simplifying the teaching and learning biology in schools and universities as well as the use of molecular biology tools in the dynamic agricultural world to promote sustainable development, with a strong bias in achieving food security in sub-Saharan Africa (essytoili@gmail.com).

# 1

# CHAPTER 1

# MEANING OF ENVIRONMENTAL EDUCATION

## Introduction

This chapter introduces the growth and development of environmental education as a substantive field of knowledge. You will be able to understand how the term environmental education was coined from the twin words: 'environment' and 'education'. You will also get the opportunity to learn the history, philosophy, goals, objectives and guiding principles of environmental education. You will also learn that the concept of environmental education has changed since the onset of education for sustainable development early in the 21$^{st}$ century.

## Expected Learning Outcomes

By the end of this chapter you should be able to:

- Demonstrate the ability to define the terms 'environment', 'environmental education' and 'environmental education for sustainability';

A section of a polluted village in Hon Tre Island, Vietnam. The environment is about the surrounding conditions which influence behaviour and development patterns of living things. Photo/LUCA FECAROTTA/FLICKR

- Discuss the major reasons for the emergence of environmental education;
- Identify the historical milestones in the development of environmental education;
- Demonstrate the ability to articulate the underlying philosophy of environmental education;
- Outline the goals and objectives of environmental education; and
- Outline the guidelines necessary in the development of curriculum and programmes in environmental education.

## Definitions of Environment and Environmental Education

### Definition of Environment

Environmental education is best understood if we first comprehend what the terms 'environment' and 'education mean'. The term environment comes from the French word *'environmer'*, meaning surrounding. The human environment is that part of the Earth we occupy and it's made up of all we can see and much that we cannot see when we look around

A few environmental activists in Canada during a sensitisation campaign in 2007. Globally, governments are grappling with ways of achieving a better environment. Photo/RODNEY HAYDEN/FLICKR

ourselves. Examples include air, soil, water, climate, buildings, other living institutions, beliefs and customs, political systems and institutions.

The above attributes can be further categorised into three, which are sometimes referred to as components of the environment. These include the natural environment, built environment, and social environment. These are further elaborated below.

## Natural Environment

The natural environment consists of the physical and naturally occurring attributes which include the following:

- Air or atmosphere;
- Climate;
- Water/hydrosphere;
- Soil/lithosphere;
- Physical features such mountains, hills, valleys, plateaus, spurs, etc;
- Plants (flora); and
- Animals (fauna).

The above features (i – v) are called *abiotic factors*, while (vi - vii) are called *biotic factors* of the environment.

## Social Environment

The social environment consists of the dimensions which arise from human interactions and include the following:

- Culture and cultural practices;
- Beliefs and customs;
- Attitudes-influenced by culture; an integral part of beliefs and customs;
- Race;
- Gender;
- Language;
- Social institutions and systems;
- Political systems and institutions; and
- Economic systems and institutions.

## Built Environment

Built environment consists of all manmade constructions such as buildings, telephone wires, electricity wires, roads, railways, bridges, movable machines, and immovable machines (factories).

## Locational terms with reference to the Environment

In terms of our location in the environment, the following terms are usually used:

- Local environment;
- National environment; and
- Global environment.

The term *local environment* refers to the area you usually stay and you are therefore familiar with. Such an area consists of land and all physical features, water, air or atmosphere, buildings and other manmade features, people and other living things (flora and fauna), and the neighbourhood.

The term *national environment* refers to all components of the environment within the borders of our country, which comprises of many local environments.

*Global environment* refers to the world environment; the entire Planet Earth. The earth is our environment in the universe.

*CONCEPT IN DEPTH*

*We can see that the term 'environment' does not just refer to the natural or physical attributes we usually see around us. It also refers to the social attributes that result from human interactions. The environment then means the surrounding conditions which influence behaviour and development patterns of living things. It is therefore defined as the sum total of the physical, chemical, biological, social, economic, political, aesthetic, and structural surroundings of humankind.*

## Definition of Environmental Education

We have already defined the term 'environment'. We must now define the term 'environmental education'. This involves a recapitulation of the terms environment and education. Environment refers to the sum total of the physical, chemical, biological, social, economic, political, aesthetic, and structural surroundings of humankind. On the other hand, 'Education' is seen as a process of developing in an individual certain knowledge, skills, attitudes and values by means of which one identifies with their society and actively participates in the development of the society.

Environmental Education (EE) is, therefore, the process of developing in an individual the knowledge, skills, attitudes and values that will enable one to interact fruitfully and live in harmony with the conditions that surround them. The most widely used definition was reached in 1970 at the International Workshop on Environmental Education held in Nevada; USA organised by the International Union for Conservation of Nature and Natural Resources (IUCN). The workshop gave the following definition of EE (UNESCO, 1980):

> *EE is the process of recognising values and clarifying concepts in order to develop skills and attitudes necessary to understand and appreciate the interrelations between man, his culture and his biophysical surroundings. It also entails practice in decision making and formulation of a code of behaviour about issues concerning the environmental quality.*

From the definition, EE is seen as a process aimed at developing a world population that is aware of and concerned about the total environment and its associated problems and which has the knowledge, skills, attitudes and commitment to work individually and collectively towards the resolution of current problems and prevention of new ones in order to sustain the quality of human life and that of the environment.

## Box 1.1

### Discussion Questions

*Can you now answer this question: 'Do all the elements of the environment stay the same'?* You may now think of an answer like this one: The basic features of the Earth stay the same, but the details of each are constantly changing. This is attributed to our daily activities which change various elements or components of the environment. However, the details of each of these elements have over the years changed leading to various environmental problems, a situation commonly referred to as an ***environmental crisis.***

## History and Philosophy of Environmental Education

As with any other field of knowledge, it is important to know how and when environmental education started (the history). We need to know what it stands for (its philosophy)? Every area of knowledge has its own history. The sub-sections below outline how environmental education started and the major milestones realised in relation to its development and progress. The philosophy of environmental education is also articulated.

During the 1960s and early 1970s, many voices were raised in alarm against the rapid deterioration of the global environment. To prevent any further destruction of the global environment it was found necessary to sensitise all the people throughout the world against misuse and abuse of their environments.

A general view of the opening meeting of the UN Conference at the Folkets Hus, Stockholm in June 1972. Photo/UNITED NATIONS

This dream was realised when in 1972 the international community converged at the United Nations Conference on the Human Environment (UNCHE) held in Stockholm, Sweden. The conference mooted the idea of environmental education. It also recommended that the United Nations Environmental Education Programme (UNEP) be created to coordinate all matters relating to the global environment. The programme was established in 1973 with its headquarters in Nairobi, Kenya.

The UNEP in conjunction with UNESCO later founded the International Environmental Education Programme (IEEP) which was charged with the responsibility of developing and coordinating all environmental education programmes the world over. The IEEP was launched at the International Workshop on Environmental Education (IWEE) held in Belgrade in Yugoslavia in 1975. The workshop developed the Belgrade Charter in which the aims, objectives, key concepts and guiding principles of environmental education were spelt out.

In October 1977, UNEP and UNESCO organised the Intergovernmental Conference on Environmental Education (IGCEE) held in Tbilisi, Georgia in the then Union of Soviet Socialist Republics (USSR). The conference discussed and refined the aims, objectives, key concepts and guiding principles of environmental education contained in the Belgrade Charter. All countries of the world were urged to introduce it in their curricula at all levels of education, using the guidelines that were developed at the conference. This was the beginning of modern environmentalism.

The progress of environmental education was evaluated at Tbilisi Plus Ten Conference held in Moscow in 1987 and at the United Nations Conference on Environment and Development (UNCED), also referred to as the Earth Summit held in Rio de Janeiro in 1992. It was found that not much had been achieved in its implementation in most countries. At the Rio de Janeiro summit, it was recommended, in Agenda 21, that environmental education be incorporated as an essential part of learning at all levels of education within three years.

A follow-up discussion on Agenda 21 (Chapter 36 on Education, Public Awareness and Training) was done at the International Conference on Environment and Society held in Thessaloniki, Greece. It focused on the role of environmental education in fostering sustainable development. The idea of education for sustainability was born and a proposal for the establishment of a conceptual framework for Education for Sustainability (ESD) within the context of environmental education was made.

In 2000, the Earth Charter was launched at The Hague, Netherlands. This was a civil call for sustainability and a declaration of fundamental principles for building a just, sustainable and peaceful society in the 21st century, based on respect for nature, diversity, universal human rights, economic justice and a culture of peace. The charter sets forth a concise formulation of the meaning of sustainable living and development. The Charter provides an elaboration on the dimensions of the human environment and sustainable development that should be covered in environmental education for sustainability. The participants in implementing the charter should include students, governments, leaders, local authorities, communities and international agencies. It is a living charter with the power to unite people for a common purpose: care and concern for the whole community.

The World Summit on Sustainable Development (WSSD) was then held in Johannesburg in 2002 to enhance the implementation of the resolutions on sustainable development by governments. To provide the momentum for this, the United Nations Decade of Education for Sustainable Development (UNDESD) was declared to cover the period

2005-2014. Environmental Education for Sustainability is now the agenda for education at all levels and across all sectors. The 4th International Conference on Environmental Education held in Ahmadabad, India, in 2007 provided further momentum on the achievement of sustainable development through the provisions of UNDESD.

Environmental education is rooted in a clear philosophy - a system of beliefs, ideology or convictions about living -from which ethical or moral principles and values are extracted to serve as its desired goals. The underlying philosophy should be characterised by a world citizen who is self-disciplined and possesses personal ethics with regard to the environment.

Self-discipline leads to a balanced personality capable of using energy, knowledge, and wealth sparingly and for the purpose of improving the quality of human life and that of the environment that provides the wealth. The lack of it is one reason why man became threatened by the very things he valued most: power, mastery over nature, the scientific addition of knowledge (Mumford, 1944). We desire a disciplined world citizen who acts as a guardian of the planet by developing and using requisite skills to protect and improve it. In making personal life plans, such an individual would be guided by a personal ethic. As a guardian of the planet, one would ensure that one's choices will add enrichment to humankind as a whole. This would entail participating in activities that put an end to social ills such as poverty, hunger, illiteracy, pollution, exploitation and domination. This would also entail examining development activities to ensure they do not adversely affect the quality of the environment. The citizen should participate in protecting and improving the quality of the environment.

The call for environmental education is, therefore, a call for global action in response to the problem of the abused environments – physical and social. This requires a world citizen who shares a concern for the environment in which they now live and in which their descendants will also have to live. The beliefs and attitudes which characterise the world citizen and which should, therefore, serve as the underlying philosophy of EE are twofold:

- The world citizen should develop personal ethics that includes a global dimension. The global dimension demands that each world citizen see oneself as a guardian of the national and international good, developing and using the skills of negotiation and compromise to resolve situations of conflict. This means abandoning previously accepted priorities and activities that destroy

9

the environment and taking on better ways of interacting with the environment; and

- Every world citizen should develop a personal ethic that includes a global dimension. Economic activities done to raise the quality of life should also sustain the quality of the environment on which the activities are based (sustainable development). The tenets of this new philosophy are spelt out in the Belgrade Charter 1975):

*To develop a world population that is aware of and concerned about the environment and its associated problems, and which has the knowledge, skills, attitudes, motivations and commitment to work individually and collectively toward solutions of current problems and the prevention of new ones.*

---

**Box 1.2**

---

### Discussion

Are you now able to state the philosophy of environmental education? It should be clear to you that environmental education hopes to help human beings realise meaning, happiness, and transcendence in their lives by embracing the spirit of stewardship. In this way, they learn to survive, flourish, and do work on this Earth without adversely affecting the quality of our lives and that of the environment. The tenets of this new philosophy are succinctly expressed in the goals, objectives and guiding principles of environmental education.

---

## Goals, Objectives and Guiding Principles of Environmental Education

The goals, objectives and guiding principles of environmental education outlined here are those that were agreed upon at the Tbilisi conference in 1977 and are indicated as Recommendation No. 2 of the conference. These are now outlined as follows:

The ultimate goals of EE are:

- To foster clear awareness of and concern about, economic, social, political and ecological interdependence in urban and rural areas;
- To provide every person with opportunities to acquire the knowledge, values, attitudes, commitment and skills needed to protect and improve the environment; and
- To create new patterns of behaviour of individuals, groups and society as a whole towards the environment.

## Objectives

The objectives of environmental education are to develop the following qualities in individuals and social groups:

- Awareness of, and sensitivity to, the total environment and its problems (*environmental awareness*);
- Social values and feelings of concern for the environment and motivation for active participation in environmental protection and improvement (*environmental attitudes)*;
- Experience in, and a basic understanding of, the environment and its problems *(environmental knowledge)*;
- Skills for identifying and solving environmental problems (environmental skills); and
- Active participation at all levels in working toward resolution of environmental problems (*environmental action and participation).*

## Guiding Principles

To achieve the objectives environmental education should:

- Consider the environment in its totality - natural, built, technological and social;
- Be a continuous lifelong process;
- Be interdisciplinary in its approach, drawing on the specific content of each discipline in making possible a holistic and balanced perspective;
- Examine major environmental issues from local, national, regional, and international points of view so that students receive insights into environmental conditions in other geographical areas;
- Focus on current and potential environmental situations while taking into account the historical perspective;

- Promote the value and necessity of local, national, and international cooperation in the prevention and solution of environmental problems;
- Relate environmental sensitivity, knowledge, problem-solving skills and values clarification to every age, but with special emphasis on environmental sensitivity to the learner's own community in early years;
- Help learners discover the symptoms and real causes of environmental problems;
- Emphasise the complexity of environmental problems and thus the need to develop critical thinking and problem-solving skills; and
- Utilise diverse learning environments and a broad array of educational approaches to teaching and learning about, from and for the environment with due stress on practical activities and firsthand experiences.

**Work to do:**

Imagine that you have been asked by your principal to develop an environmental education programme for your school.

- Outline the objectives for the programme you may develop; and
- Indicate the guiding principles that you will employ for the process.

**Do you know?**

Only through our actions will our children inherit a world full of dignity and decency free of poverty, environmental degradation and unsustainable consumption of resources. To achieve sustainable development, effective, democratic and accountable institutions must be established.

Box 1.3

Discussion

Are you now in a position to differentiate between environmental education and environmental education for sustainability? It is important to note at this moment that there is no better vehicle for taking us to the attainment of more ecologically, economically, politically and socially sustainable development than environmental education for sustainability.

---

## Summary

In this chapter, you have learned about the perspectives of environmental education. This involved definitions of environment and environmental education, and the historical growth and development as well as the philosophy of environmental education. It was evident that environmental education is all about attempting to understand the dynamic intricacies of the environment and what we can do to safeguard its quality, while its philosophy is embedded in our own individual discipline as expressed in our ability to be good stewards of the environment.

You have also learned that environmental education has distinct goals, objectives and guiding principles which were established at the Tbilisi conference in 1977. The goals provide the broad outcomes of environmental education in terms of knowledge, skills and attitudes. The objectives are the specific outcomes for each of the goals in terms of raising awareness and understanding about the environment, developing feelings of concern about the quality of the environment, developing skills of identifying and solving problems related to the environment, and acquiring action and participation skills for improving the quality of the environment.

Finally, you learned that the focus of environmental education has shifted to sustainable development, and it's now being referred to as environmental education for sustainability. The scope of environmental education under the new focus has expanded to include safeguarding the quality of the environment in terms of social, ecological, economic and political dimensions.

## End of Chapter Self-Test Questions

Answer all of the following questions:

Question 1

    a) List the three components of the environment.
    b) Provide four examples for each of the components in (a) above.

Question 2

    a) In less than 20 words, provide the definition of environmental education------------------------------------------------------------------------

---------------------------------------------------------------
---------------------------------------------------------------
---------------------------------------------------------------
---------------------------------------------------------------

## Question 3

a) Copy and complete the table below, indicating the major milestones in the growth and development of environmental education. The first row has been completed for you as an example.

| Year | Activity | Achievement |
|------|----------|-------------|
| 1970 | Workshop on Environmental Education, held in Nevada, USA | The first definition of environmental education given |
| 1972 | | |
| 1975 | | |
| 1977 | | |
| 1980 | | |
| 1992 | | |
| 1997 | | |
| 2002 | | |

## Question 4

a) In not more than 15 words outline the philosophy of environmental education----------------------------------------------------
---------------------------------------------------------------
---------------------------------------------------------------

Question 5

   a)  Explain briefly the tenets of the objectives of environmental
       education.

Question 6

   a)  List the four critical dimensions in sustainable development
   b)  Give the major differences between environmental education and
       environmental education for sustainability
   c)  Provide any three reasons why environmental education for
       sustainability is necessary

## Bibliography

Korir- Koech, M (1988): Environmental Education PAC 101 Faculty of
       External Degree Studies, University of Nairobi.
Muyanda-Mutebi, P(Ed) Environmental Education: A Teaching and
       Training Guide Pan Africa Books.
Muthoka, M, Rego and Rimbui, Z (1998) Environmental Education:
       Essential knowledge for Sustainable Development Longhorn
UNESCO (1980): Environmental Education in the Light of Tbilisi
       Conference.
Otiende, J.E. et al. (1991): Environmental Education Nairobi University
       Press

# 2

## CHAPTER 2

# THE EARTH'S ENVIRONMENT: DELICATE BALANCE OF NATURE

Introduction

This chapter focuses on the Earth's environment. In this chapter, you will learn about the nature of the natural environment provided by the planet Earth. You will learn about the various components of the Earth's environment including ecological systems and natural resources. You will notice that all components of the environment occur in a balanced manner. In this balance, you will be able to understand how the sun provides the original source of energy that all living things depend on and how the energy flows in the ecosystems. Of particular significance, you will learn that the flow of energy in ecosystems is not very efficient, making the conservation of energy and other resources necessary. The role of humankind in the stability of ecosystems will also be explained to you.

Mt Kenya glaciers are slowly fading away. Photo/DAVID HAMILL/FLICKR

**Expected Learning Outcomes**

By the end of this topic you should be able to:

- Describe the spheres of the earth's environment;
- Identify the zones of the atmosphere and state their functions;
- Explain why the earth is regarded as spaceship earth;
- Define the term ecosystem and describe the major features of ecosystems;
- Discuss the efficiency of energy transfer in ecosystems; and
- Provide evidence to illustrate the natural balance in ecosystems.

## Spaceship Earth: Its Environment

Earth is the only planet where life exists. As you may be aware, the Earth is about six billion years old. It is a small spherical body among the thousands of planets, stars and galaxies, which stretch greater distances than we can ever imagine. But this small sphere is the only planet where life exists. It is our environment in which we live. The Earth's environment has two interacting components that make life possible. These are Atmosphere and

Biosphere. We shall now briefly discuss each of them to understand how they are able to support life.

## The Atmosphere

The atmosphere is a mixture of gases held close to the Earth's surface by the force of gravity. This mixture forms a blanket or envelope around the earth's surface.

The atmosphere spreads high above the earth for several hundreds of kilometres (up to about 900 kilometres). It is thicker near the earth's surface and gets thinner as it gets higher e.g. one finds it difficult to breathe at the top of Mt. Kenya because there is not just enough air in the atmosphere at the top of the mountain, for above the mountain, the atmosphere becomes thinner and thinner until it melts into space. There is no air in space.

## Composition of the atmosphere

The gases that form the atmosphere are invisible and are delicately balanced in different proportions by volume as shown in Table 2.1

**Table 2.1 Atmospheric Gases by Volume**

| GAS | AVERAGE % BY VOLUME |
| --- | --- |
| Nitrogen | 78.8 |
| Oxygen | 20.9 |
| Carbon Dioxide | 0.03 |
| Inert Gases | |
|    a) Argon | 0.93 |
|    b) Neon | 0.0018 |
|    c) Helium | 0.00052 |
| Trace Gases e.g. hydrogen, methane, Carbon monoxide e.t.c | < 0.0001 |
| Water Vapour | Variable (1-4%) |

Because the Earth has pre-determined requirements in definite proportions it acts as a spaceship, therefore it is referred to as *spaceship earth*. The atmospheric composition must remain the same. If it is changed, there will be far-reaching consequences to the earth and its inhabitants.

The atmosphere consists of components or zones (Figure 2.1) each with specific functions that make life possible on Earth. These zones include the Troposphere, Stratosphere, Mesosphere, Thermosphere and Magnetosphere.

## Troposphere

This is the lowest region of the atmosphere. It is in contact with the surface of the earth. It is found within a height of between 8 - 15 km. It consists of about 80% of the components of the atmosphere. It contains varying quantities of dust and water vapour. Such features of the weather as clouds, storms, wind, fog, precipitation are found in this zone. The temperature decreases with height at an average of 1°c for every 165m.

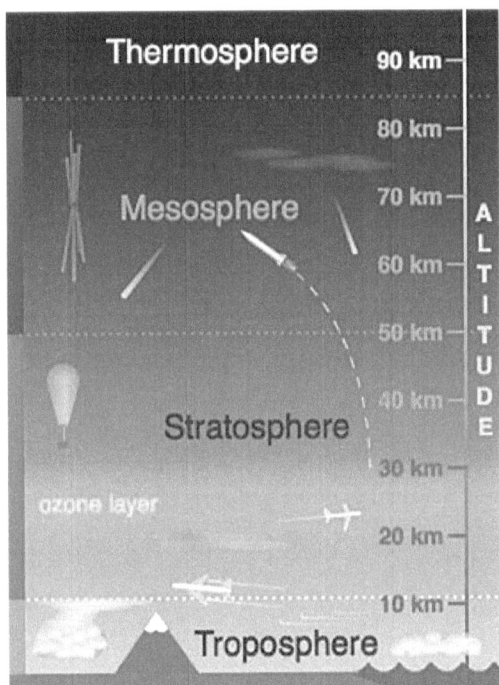

## Stratosphere

This zone extends between 20 - 50 km. It contains an ozone layer that shields the surface of the earth from dangerous radiation of the sun particularly ultraviolet and x-rays. The ozone layer is formed when the oxygen in this region absorbs ultraviolet light. The oxygen molecules are broken down into its atoms, some oxygen atoms then join oxygen molecules to give $O_3$ molecules.

Layers of the atmosphere: troposphere, stratosphere, mesosphere and thermosphere. Graphics/RANDY RUSSELL/UCAR

As $O_3$ molecules are being formed, others are combining with $O_2$ atoms to give oxygen molecules, hence the situation is one of the equilibria with $O_3$ being formed and destroyed at the same time. About 99% of the U.V. radiation does not reach the Earth's surface because of this absorption.

19

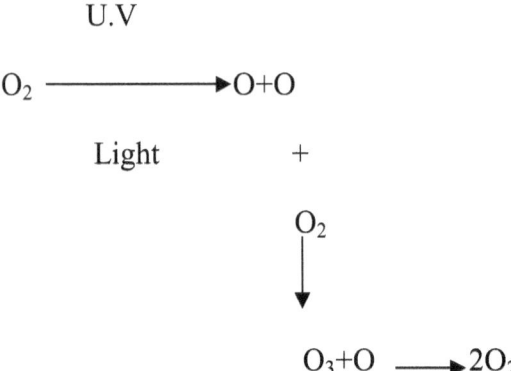

## Mesosphere

This region extends between 50 - 80 km above the Earth's surface. It consists of less gaseous mass; and has no water vapour. The temperature falls up to -75°c. The upper mesosphere has electrically charged particles and it is part of the ionosphere- where things exist as ions.

## Thermosphere

This zone extends from 80 - 900km above earth's surface. Temperature increases up to 2000°c. It lacks water vapour, oxygen and ozone. However, it has abundant electrically charged particles. Together with the upper level of the mesosphere, the region forms the ionosphere. This region reflects radio waves back to the earth's surface and enables wireless communication to work effectively.

## Magnetosphere

This layer is located beyond the limits of the atmosphere and it is found around and beyond 950km above the Earth' surface. A magnetic field exists which traps magnetic particles contained in the solar radiation.

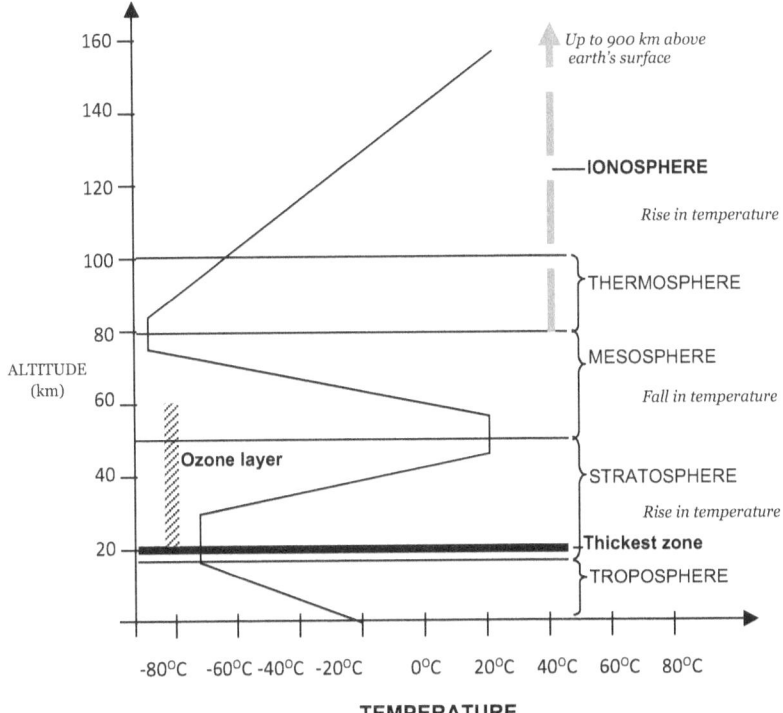

**Figure 2.1: Atmospheric Zones**

Functions of the atmosphere:

- It provides oxygen, which is used by living things during respiration, thus sustaining their lives;
- It provides carbon dioxide, used by plants to synthesise their own food during photosynthesis. It traps some of the sunlight energy, which is absorbed by the plant during this process;
- Some of the light rays reflected back to the atmosphere by the earth's surface helps in regulating the global temperature - the moon and other planets are very cold because they do not have the atmosphere to help regulate the temperature. The regulation of the temperature is achieved through the "GREENHOUSE EFFECT";
- It is responsible for the blue colour of the sky. It also forms the colours of the sunrise and sunset and for the rainbow; and
- The atmosphere shields us against harmful rays of the sun such as

gamma rays, x-rays, x-particles and U.V rays. These are usually blocked, absorbed or reflected back by the upper layers of the atmosphere particularly the ozone layer.

## The Biosphere (Sphere of Life)

It is a very thin layer of the earth's crust consisting of Soil, Water, and Lower levels of the atmosphere (Troposphere). Life on earth only occurs within the biosphere. Only a few specialised animals have ever moved outside the biosphere i.e. man, birds and insects. The biosphere consists of three components, namely:

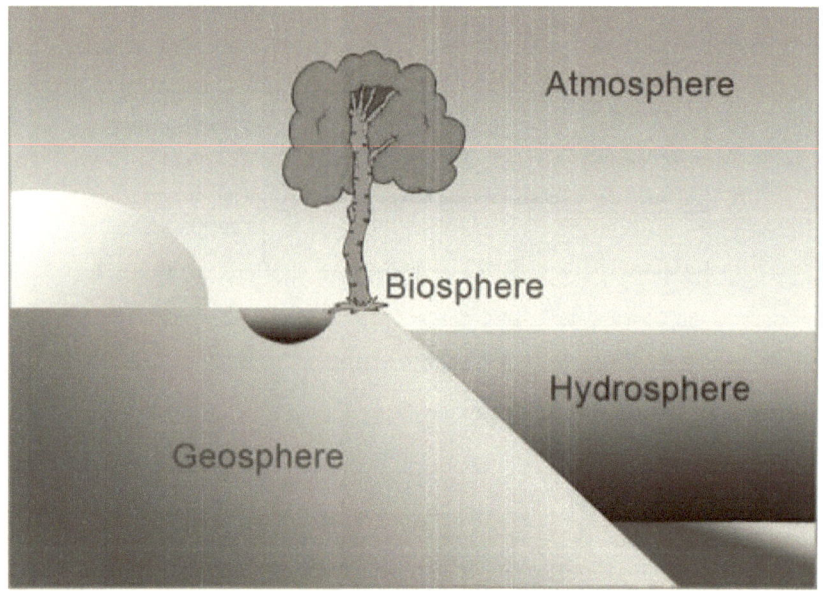

A diagram of the Biosphere. Graphics/PINTEREST

- Lithosphere;
- Hydrosphere; and
- Troposphere.

The lithosphere is the abiotic component of the earth's environment (non-living part). It is found a few meters below the ground and as far as the deepest roots can go ($\cong$1km). While our heads spend most of their time in the atmosphere our feet are usually planted on the earth's rocky outer crust i.e. lithosphere

The lithosphere consists of soil, minerals and surface layer of the rocks that are directly involved in the life processes. Some of the minerals found in the lithosphere include silicon, aluminium, iron, calcium, sodium, potassium, and magnesium. Oxygen is also found in the lithosphere. Other features of the lithosphere include continents, plains and plateaus, hills and valleys.

The lithosphere is of great significance because of its soil cover, which is indispensable for the growth of plants, which in turn provide food for man and other animal life.

## Hydrosphere

The hydrosphere is made up of all types of water bodies – oceans, seas, lakes, rivers, streams, reservoirs, glaciers, and others on earth including underground water. The most important part is the top 150m of the water in the oceans, lakes, rivers, seas, and underground water.

## Troposphere

Only a part of it is important for life particularly the few meters above the treetops where gaseous exchange takes place. This exchange brings about the weather changes we always observe such as condensation, precipitation, wind movement and cloud formation.

## Box 2.1

### Discussion

It is important to note the following points in relation to this section:

- Plant and animal life (biotic component) is found mainly in the lithosphere and hydrosphere. Several specialised animals are also found in the atmosphere e.g. birds, bats and insects;
- The location of a plant or an animal in these zones (litho or hydrosphere) is called habitat (home);
- A group of animals and plants living in a particular habitat forms a community;
- Plants or animals of the same kind are called species; and
- Today, the biosphere consists of about one million plant species and two million animal species, thus animals are more than plants.

However, plants are more dominant.

---

## Ecosystems: Nature's Web

### Definition of Ecosystem

Plants and animals (biotic environment) interact with the soil, water and air (the biotic environment) in the biosphere. The biosphere can, therefore, be regarded as an ecological system. However, it is rather too large and complex to be a useful or a manageable unit of study. Such interaction is best observed or studied at the ecosystem level.

An *ecosystem* is a small unit of the biosphere where living and non-living things of the environment interact to form a stable and self-regulating system. An ecosystem is thus, a complex, self–perpetuating community of living things together with the non-living environment in a given area. Examples of the ecosystem include pond, dam, tree, swamp, lake, sea, river, building and graveyard.

Each ecosystem has three components – plants, animals and the non-living part.

---

**Box 2.2**

---

*Discussion*

Note that:

- A large ecosystem is called a biome, e.g. tropical rainforest, tundra region, temperate rainforest, savannah grassland, desert, coniferous forest. Biomes are usually named after the main type of vegetation found there and each one is home to a large variety of plants and animals;
- The largest ecosystem that ecologists study is the biosphere; and
- The earth's biosphere contains many ecosystems within each ecosystem are habitats. Each habitat contains smaller microenvironments; each with its non-abiotic conditions.

---

Living things in an ecosystem are linked to another by feeding relationship. These relationships include food chains and food webs. The primary purpose of the feeding relationships is to transfer the energy and the materials required by all living organisms in carrying out their daily functions.

## Food Chains

A food chain is the simplest feeding relationship in any ecosystem. A food chain is a series of organisms where each one is dependent on the one preceding it for its source of energy and essential nutrients (Figure 2.2). In a food chain, each food link represents a trophic level. The first link is composed of green plants or primary producers. They manufacture their own food during the process of photosynthesis. Plants are in turn eaten by herbivores (primary consumers). In turn, the herbivores may be eaten by a carnivore (i.e. secondary consumer). In a long food chain, there may be carnivores, which feed on other carnivores hence called tertiary consumers omnivores are also tertiary consumers.

Each food chain also contains decomposers which break down dead plant and animal matter into minerals (humus) which are then returned to the soil to be used again. This process is called decay and decomposition. The decomposers include bacteria, fungi, and some arthropods. An example of a food chain is indicated in Figure 2.2

An infographic showing producers and consumers in a food chain. Graphics/BBC

In a natural ecosystem, there are usually not more than 4 or 5 trophic levels in a food chain. The limits are imposed by the energy losses between one trophic level and the next combined with the fact that energy requirements may increase as one goes up the trophic levels.

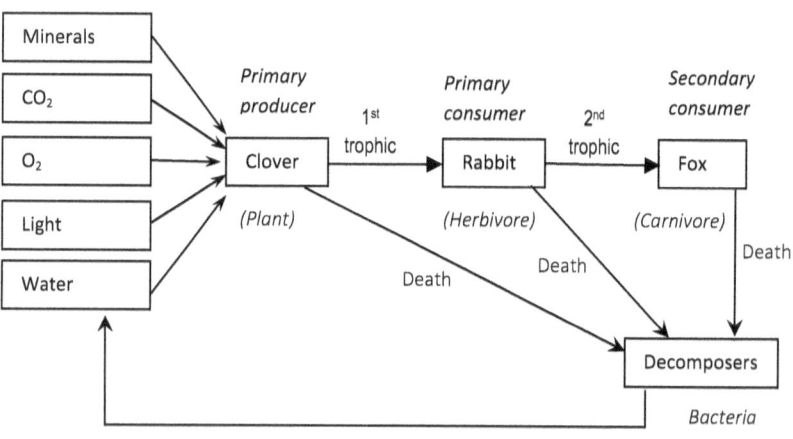

**Fig 2.2: An Example of Food Chain**

In the natural ecosystems, simple food chains rarely exist, instead, chains join together into more complex relationships known as food webs. This is because animals often eat a varied diet and so play different roles in a number of food chains. An example of a food web is shown in Figure 2.3.

If any one element is missing in the food chain, the food chain is broken and the whole community is affected e.g. foxes will die due to starvation if there are no mice and chicks. Also, if one group increases in number the whole community is affected in some way as the carrying capacity are affected. But left undisturbed, nature keeps the balance within a given ecosystem.

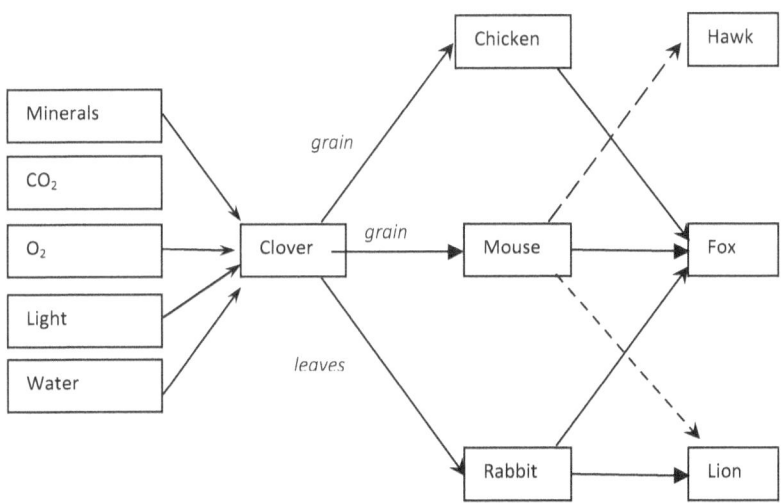

**Figure 2.3: An Example of Food Web**

Energy Flow in Ecosystems

Energy is the ability to work, and all organisms need a source of energy to live. In an ecosystem, living things obtain this energy from food, i.e. chemical energy. The food is also used by living organisms for growth and repair of worn-out tissues. Overall, living things in an ecosystem are linked to one another by food energy or chemical energy.

The initial source of energy for any ecosystem is the sun (solar energy). Green plants have chlorophyll in the leaves which traps solar energy from the sun and use it to convert water from the soil, carbon dioxide from the atmosphere and small amount or traces of minerals dissolved in soil water into high energy compounds mainly carbohydrates (primary productivity).

$$6CO_2 + 6H_2O \xrightarrow[\text{Chlorophyll}]{\text{Light Energy}} C_6H_{12}O_6 + 6O_2$$

Low chemical                                    High chemical

Energy                                          Energy

Much of the energy contained in carbohydrates is released during respiration and used in the plant to build larger molecules such as cellulose, starch, oil and proteins. As the plant synthesises these materials, it increases in size (plant biomass) and an increased amount of energy is stored within it. This energy stored in the plant structure is available to animals, which eat them.

Also, when plants die, the energy is made available as dead organic matter. The process of respiration also releases the energy in plant materials, eaten by animals. During this process, the organic substances in the food are broken down with the help of oxygen to release energy. The process is chemically a reverse of photosynthesis.

$$C_6H_{12}O_6 + 6O_2 \longrightarrow 6CO_2 + 6H_2O + \text{Heat energy (2.8ml)}$$

The animals, in turn, use the energy released to:

- Synthesise materials necessary to keep them healthy or for the purpose of growth. Energy is in turn stored in the animal material or tissues i.e. animal biomass; and
- Perform various life processes such as movement, transport of materials in the body e.t.c.

Most of the light energy that falls onto a plant is reflected again into the atmosphere. Only about 1% is clearly absorbed by plants to provide chemical energy as indicated in Figure 2.4.

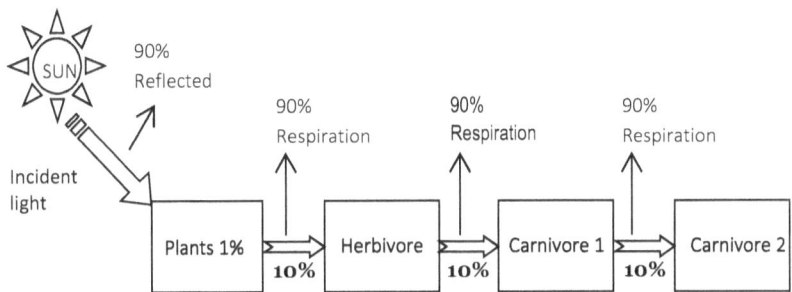

**Figure 2.4: Energy Transfer in Food Chains**

On the other hand, of the chemical energy produced in the plant, in the form of food or plant materials, only 10% is used by the herbivores or primary consumers and is fixed in their flesh. The other 90% is lost as heat during respiration as shown in Figure 2.5. The same is true when a herbivore is eaten by a carnivore or carnivore is eaten by another carnivore. Thus, only 10% of the energy at the trophic level is subsequently fixed in the tissues of the succeeding level. The system is thus highly inefficient hence we cannot have more than five trophic levels in a food chain in an ecosystem, hence, the need to conserve the environment.

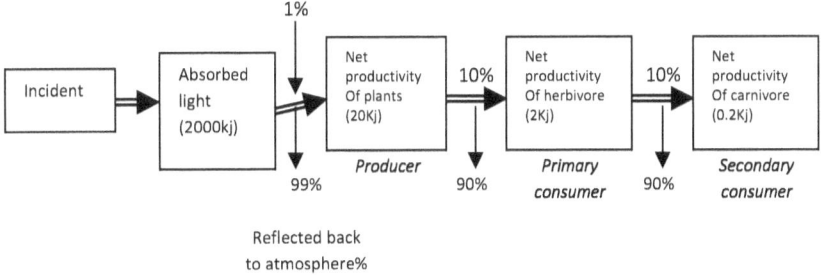

**Figure 2.5: Efficiency of Energy Transfer in Food Chains**

Because of the energy losses at each trophic level, any producer can only produce enough chemical energy to support a smaller number of organisms in the chain. Hence, the amount of animal biomass that can be supported at each succeeding trophic level decreases at a geometric rate in an ecosystem. This explains why a food chain rarely exceeds 4 or 5 trophic levels. The dissipation of heat (loss) results in an energy deficit. A constant infusion of additional energy is required for ecosystems to continue functioning and for organisms to live and grow. The sun provides this constant supply of energy.

Similarly, inorganic materials must also continually be supplied to help in the productivity of materials in plants and subsequently in animals. These inorganic materials are supplied through biological cyclings such as carbon, nitrogen and water cycle.

## The Natural Balance in Ecosystems

The biosphere has a countless number of ecosystems consisting of plants, animals and non- living things. All these components of the ecosystems are in a closely balanced order. There is no waste and everything is broken down and reused. The ability of an ecosystem to support a certain number of plants and animals is referred to as its *carrying capacity.* The natural balance is at two levels i.e. Biotic balance, and Abiotic balance. These two levels are now briefly discussed.

### Biotic Balance

It is evident from food chains, food webs and energy flow in ecosystems that if any feeding level is changed, the ecosystem is thrown out of balance. This is because the carrying capacity of the ecosystems is affected by such changes. All ecosystems have inbuilt mechanisms for regulating the balance mainly through photosynthesis, respiration, and decomposition. The biotic balance of an ecosystem is usually expressed in ecological and energy pyramids.

### Ecological Pyramids

There are two types of ecological pyramids:

- Pyramid of numbers; and
- Pyramid of biomass

### Pyramid of numbers

As we progress along a food chain, the numbers of individual representatives of each tropic level are grouped together in a block that may be drawn to indicate the total number of organisms in the chain such as Figure 2.6. However, it is difficult to use a pyramid of numbers to compare different ecosystems. For example, at the producer level, it is pointless to compare organisms which are vastly different in sizes such as an alga and a tree as seen in Figure 2.7.

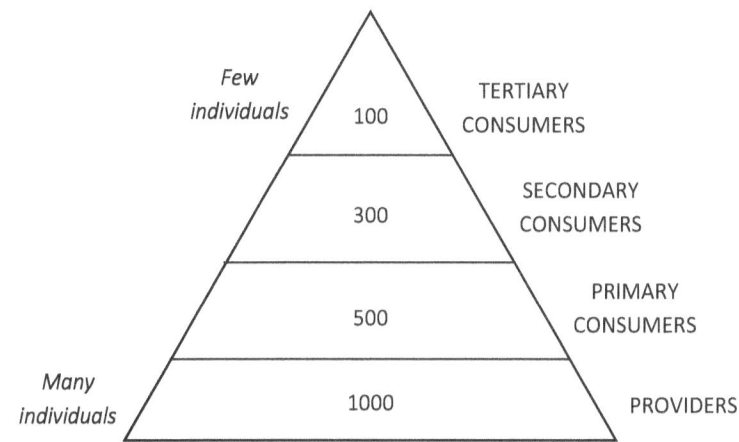

**Figure 2.6: Representation of Regular Pyramid of Numbers**

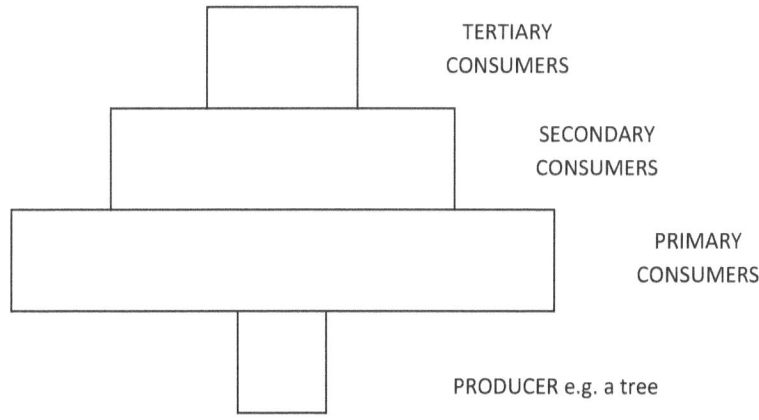

**Figure 2.7: Representation of Special Type of Pyramid of Numbers**

Pyramid of Biomass

Pyramid of biomass is based on the dry mass of organisms found at each trophic level. Instead of counting numbers in an ecosystem, the mass of an organism is considered and it is used to construct a pyramid of biomass.

The majority of pyramids of biomass take the same shape as that pyramid of numbers (see Figure 2.8).

However, this approach has two key limitations. First, the pyramid of biomass samples the mass of organisms at one particular time not taking into account the variations over time, the lifespan of the organisms involved or the rate of growth and reproduction of the organisms. More so, they may need to collect these organisms for the purpose of determining their dry weight thus interfering with the ecosystem.

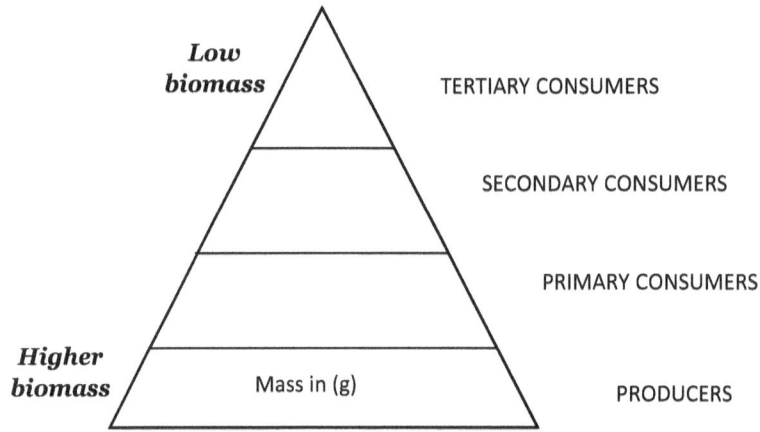

**Figure 2.8: Representation of Pyramid of Biomass**

Energy Pyramids

The energy utilised by different feeding types in a unit area over a period of time (usually a year) can be used to construct pyramids. The pyramid overcomes the difficulties of comparison of ecosystems arising from different sizes of organisms and the differences in energy equivalent of unit masses of tissues (Figure 2.9). Energy pyramids are the best measure of the energy conservation of the ecosystem and therefore the efficiency of ecosystems.

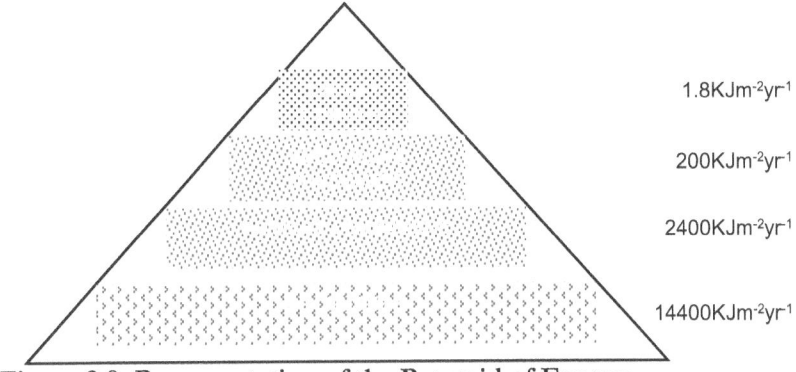

Figure 2.9: Representation of the Pyramid of Energy

Abiotic Balance

Apart from the solar energy, all abiotic needs of living things in ecosystems are supplied from the Earth's resources contained in the biosphere. The materials include the following:

- 20 chemical elements or nutrients needed by plants in large quantities (macronutrients) e.g. $O_2$, N, $H_2$, C, P, Ca, Mg, K and $S_2$. These are found within the lithosphere;
- Several other chemical elements needed by plants in smaller quantities (micronutrients) e.g. Zinc (Zn), Copper (Cu), Nickel, Iron (Fe), Boron (Bo), Manganese (Mn), Silicon (Si), Chlorine (Cl), Sodium (Na), Molybdenum (Mn). These are found within the lithosphere as well;
- Water for photosynthesis; and
- Carbon dioxide for photosynthesis.

All these materials are needed to supply energy for life and are also important in the process of growth, repair and renewal of the living cells. If these materials essential for life were only used once, they would soon run out. However, there is a constant supply of the materials between the atmosphere, lithosphere and living things through cycling. This is why many of the processes in nature work in cycles.

In any ecosystem, materials are cycled and recycled via the food chains and the food webs. When living things eventually die, decomposers convert them to inorganic or abiotic forms thus releasing the nutrients back to the lithosphere to be used. These recycling processes ensure that all living things are able to live and grow.

The inorganic or abiotic materials are continually supplied by biological cycling. Examples of these cycles include:

- Carbon cycle;
- Nitrogen cycle;
- Phosphorous cycle;
- Sulphur cycle; and
- Water cycle.

We now describe briefly the Carbon Cycle (Figure 2.10) to illustrate how this nutrient is cycled through the atmosphere, lithosphere, hydrosphere and the biotic environment.

## The Carbon Cycle

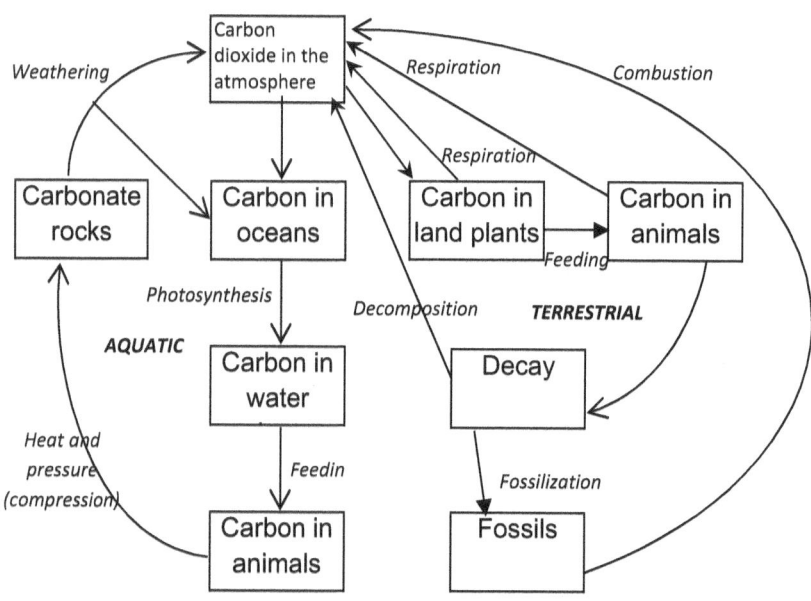

**Figure 2.10: A Representation of the Carbon Cycle**

Box 2.2

Discussion

The carbon cycle is self-regulating, but human activity is gradually upsetting the balance, mainly through the accelerated burning of vast quantities of fossil fuels and by increased deforestation.

Deforestation reduces the capacity for photosynthesis and thus a decrease in the volume of carbon dioxide removed from the atmosphere. At present carbon dioxide is being released at a rate well above that of natural cycling. If the present atmospheric levels of carbon dioxide increase by 25% this would be catastrophic.

## Summary

In this chapter, you have learned about the natural environment provided by the planet Earth. This involved an understanding of the various dimensions of the Earth's environment including the components of the atmosphere and the dynamics of ecosystems in terms of their functioning, energy flow, and natural balance.

You learned that the Earth's environment consists of three interacting spheres which make it habitable. For example, you noticed that all components of the atmosphere such as troposphere, stratosphere, and mesosphere are designed to make life possible on Earth. In terms of the functioning of ecosystems, you learned that there is a limit to the number of trophic levels beyond which the ecosystem is unable to sustain itself. You also learned that the sun provides the original source of energy that all living things depend on and that the energy flows through all the three spheres of the ecosystems. Of particular significance, you learned that the flow of energy in ecosystems is not very efficient, making the conservation of energy and other resources necessary.

Finally, you learned about the balance of nature in terms of biotic and abiotic balance. It was explained to you that materials in the environment are cycled through all its three spheres to maintain the balance. The role of humankind in the stability of ecosystems was emphasised in which it was evident that we need to conserve the resources at all costs.

## End of Chapter Self-Test Questions

Question 1

a)  List the three spheres of the environment

## Question 2

a) In less than 15 words, provide the definition of ecosystem----------

----------------------------------------------------------------------

----------------------------------------------------------------------

----------------------------------------------------------------------

## Question 3

a) State any three functions of the atmosphere----------------------------

----------------------------------------------------------------------

----------------------------------------------------------------------

----------------------------------------------------------------------

## Question 4

a) Identify and briefly describe the ways in which humankind destabilises the natural balance of ecosystems

## Question 5

a) Mention any five ways in which humankind affects the carbon cycle

## Question 6

a) Make brief notes on the Nitrogen and Water cycles

## Question 7

a) Outline how the ozone layer regenerates and sustains itself

## Question 8

a) Explain why the Planet Earth is sometimes referred to as spaceship Earth

## Question 9

a) A biology student conducted research on the efficiency of energy transfer in a grassland ecosystem consisting of hyenas, lions, zebras, antelopes, grass, vultures, and acacia trees. The results for an area of $1M^2$ were as follows:

i) Tertiary consumers     $1.8 \text{ KJM}^{-2}\text{Yr}^{-1}$

ii) Secondary consumers  $200 \text{ KJM}^{-2}\text{Yr}^{-1}$

iii) Primary consumers     $2400 \text{ KJM}^{-2}\text{Yr}^{-1}$

iv) Producers               $14400 \text{ KJM}^{-2}\text{Yr}^{-1}$

## Question 10

a) Calculate the efficiency of energy transfer of the ecosystem at each of the following trophic levels:

i) Producers- Primary consumers
ii) Primary consumers- Secondary consumers
iii) Secondary consumers - Tertiary consumers

b) If a fourth trophic level was added to the ecosystem, calculate the amount of energy that would be fixed at that level

c) An energy deficit is expected in this ecosystem. Explain how the deficit is cancelled

## Question 10

a) Suppose an ecosystem near your house consists of the following organisms nappier grass, clover, sheep, moles, cassava, hawks, white egrets, cattle, ladybirds, chicken and mongoose, construct a food web for the ecosystem

## Question 11

a) In the African traditional societies, it was taboo to eat the flesh of some animals, particularly that of carnivores. Provide a scientific explanation for this observation

## Question 12

a) List as many factors as possible that make the planet Earth habitable

## Question 13

The grass eaten by a cow has the energy in it which originated from the sun and it becomes part of the cow's flesh. The energy can be returned into the earth's system for use again

a) Describe how the sun's radiation becomes part of the grass
b) After eating the grass, how does the cow get the energy from the grass?
c) How does the energy in the cow get back into the system to be used again?
d) Express the energy relations in a, b, and c above diagrammatically

Question 14

Although the universe consists of eight planets and thousands of galaxies, life exists only on the planet earth

a) Identify and describe the fundamental features that make it possible for life to exist on planet earth
b) Describe how some of these features sustain themselves

## Bibliography

Cunningham, W.P, Cunningham M.A and Saigo, B.W (2003)
   Environmental Science: A Global Concern. McGraw-Hill.
Korir- Koech, M (1988
   Environmental Education PAC 101 Faculty of
   External Degree Studies, University of Nairobi.
Muyanda-Mutebi, P(Ed)
   Environmental Education: A Teaching and
   Training Guide Pan Africa Books.
Muthoka, M, Rego and Rimbui, Z (1998)
   Environmental  Education:
   Essential knowledge for Sustainable Development. Longhorn
Odum, E.P. (1971)
   Fundamentals of Ecology.  W.A Sanders.
Otiende, J.E. et al. (1991)
   Environmental Education Nairobi University Press
UNESCO (1980)
   Environmental Education in the Light of Tbilisi
   Conference.

# 3

# CHAPTER 3

# DEVELOPMENT AND THE EARTH'S NATURAL BALANCE

## Introduction

In the previous chapter, you learned that all components of the environment occur in a balanced manner. This ensures that the ecosystems and the quality of the environment are maintained. In this chapter, you will learn more about the way human societies have invariably affected the quality of the environment through development activities and why sustainable development must be encouraged.

**Expected Learning Outcomes**

By the end of this topic you should be able to:

- Demonstrate the ability to discuss the significance of development

A car manufacturing plant. Scholars are concerned about the abilities of developing countries in becoming industrialised nations. Photo/MIRKO TOBIAS/FLICKR

to humankind;

- Outline and discuss the various human development activities that depend on environmental resources;
- Analyse critically the impact of development activities on the Earth's natural balance and the quality of the environment; and
- Demonstrate the ability to discuss the need for sustainable development

## Meaning of Development

Development is defined as the modification of the biosphere and the application of human, financial, living and non-living resources to satisfy human needs and improve the quality of human life (World Conservation Strategy, 1980). Development is needed for several reasons such as meeting the basic needs of humanity e.g. food, clothing, shelter and source of livelihoods (jobs); to improve the quality of life for humanity in terms of literacy, life expectancy, nutrition, health, sanitation, clean water among others; and to provide energy which is an essential need. In an effort to meet these needs and aspirations, nations rely on their resource base. These resources are transformed into goods and services needed in satisfying the human needs and aspirations. The extent to which this is achieved depends on the level of energy consumption and industrialisation.

Whereas the developed countries with a high level of industrialisation can easily meet these needs, developing countries face immense challenges against industrialisation. In fact, it is believed that there is no realistic hope of developing nations reaching the present standard of living of developed nations due to certain limits to development such as low level of initial capital to develop industries, low levels of technology,

lack of adequate non-renewable resources, lack of adequate energy resources, social organisation, and the ability of the biosphere to absorb the effects of industrialisation.

Traditionally, development is seen as an index of the relative economic strengths and weaknesses of national units as measured in terms of their output, technological efficiency and level of consumption. One effective way of measuring the level of development is to consider wealth. The wealth of a country is measured in terms of its Gross National Product (GNP) per capita which is the total value of goods produced and services provided by a country in a year divided by the number of people living in that country.

Developed countries have a high GNP as compared to developing countries. They have a lot of modern industries and farming methods and generate a lot of wealth. They are rich countries (high-income earners) and people living there have a high standard of living. They have plenty of food, clean water, comfortable homes, hospitals, and schools. They own many things that make their lives comfortable like TV sets, cars, refrigerators, and washing machines, among others. On the other hand, developing countries are characterised by low or middle incomes, low standards of living, little food, and access only to poor homes, hospitals and schools. Only a few people living in cities have access to things like TV sets, cars, and refrigerators.

GNP does not, however, show the differences in wealth between people and regions within a country. It says nothing about how wealth is distributed within a country. For example, in developing countries, a large population may be involved in subsistence agriculture. They thus produce most of their own requirements and sell very little. Since GNP takes no account of the goods people consume themselves, the standard of living appears to be lower than it actually is. In addition, wealth in these countries is usually concentrated in the hands of a few people and the workers in

The streets of Nairobi, Kenya. Sustainable Development can be achieved by taking into account social, economic and ecological factors. Photo/DEBORAH/FLICKR

cities earn more than the peasants in the rural areas.

However, the increase in wealth does not necessarily mean an increase in human health and happiness. Several vices like social tensions, crime, suicides, loneliness and drug abuse all seem to be on the increase in developed countries. Development should therefore not be considered in terms of only GNP. Other criteria for development which concentrate on the quality of life rather than the level of wealth need to be embraced.

While economic growth is part of development, it cannot be a goal in itself, it cannot go on indefinitely. For development to be **sustainable** it must take account of social, economic, and ecological factors as well as living and non-living resource base. The aim of development should be to improve the quality of human life. It should enable people to realise their potential and lead lives of dignity and fulfilment. Some of the universal goals include long and healthy life; provision of quality basic services such as healthcare, education, and cultural development; access to the resources needed for a decent standard of living; political freedom, guaranteed human rights and freedom from violence; low birth, death and infant mortality rates; and a balanced proportion of people living in urban areas and those engaged in agriculture. Development is real only if it makes our lives better in all these dimensions. This means that in low-income countries economic growth is urgently needed to improve the quality of life while safeguarding the quality of the environment. In high-income countries the need is to reduce resource consumption, energy use and environmental impact while extending an acceptable quality of life to all. Development must, therefore, be defined in terms of economic growth and social transformation. This means that sustainable development should become the norm rather than the exception.

## Human Development Activities

Development activities are those which usually result in tangible human benefits. The enormous growth of the industry is the most visible result of development. It is through an industry that resources are transformed into goods and services for human consumption. The sale of these goods and services results in economic growth. The world's dominant economic systems are therefore based own two potentially self-destructive and environmentally damaging principles of consumption and growth.

The major development activities include the following:

a) Subsistence economy based on farming: This is characterised by insufficient technology and capital to process raw materials or to develop industries and services; and

b) Industry: This may be primary, secondary or tertiary industry. *Primary industry* is concerned with the exploitation of natural resources and raw materials such as agriculture, forestry, fishing and mining. *Secondary industry* deals with the manufacturing of products directly from raw materials or assembled from components produced by other secondary industries such as automobile and electronic goods manufacturing industry. The *tertiary industry* consists of jobs that provide a service but do not actually produce any goods such as health services, education, security services, government offices, insurance, tourism, management, transport, retail trade and ICT services.

Developing countries are generally more engaged in selling primary commodities in their raw or nearly raw state. It is said that when primary commodities are processed or made up into industrial products they are worth six or seven times more. Industrialisation also creates more jobs. Thus industrialisation is a significant part of economic growth. However, in an attempt for developing countries to become more industrialised, they are forced to borrow heavily from the developed countries or such other financial institutions as the World Bank to put the industries in place. This certainly increases their debt burden. In order to service the rising burden of debt, they have been forced to use more environmental resources such as forest minerals, soil mining, fish, leading to environmental deterioration. Industrialisation also contributes heavily to pollution and general deterioration of the environment. In effect, heavy industry is neither desirable nor possible. Ecologists, therefore, suggest that developing

The Mau forest in Kenya. Some developing countries are using their forest minerals to pay debts. Photo/PATRICK SHEPHERD/CIFOR/FLICKR

countries should focus more on the improvement of agricultural production and small scale industries in rural areas where most people live instead of replicating heavy industrialisation like in the developed countries. Even then safeguarding of the quality of the environment must take a centre stage.

## Impact of Development Activities on Natural Balance

Nature cycles and the biotic balance are relatively stable. Any changes that occur usually take place within certain limits, so that despite minor variations, the cycles continue and life goes on. However, man's development activities are fundamentally upsetting the fine balance of nature. While development activities such as industrial production contribute to the development of a country, the processes such as the production, transformation and final use of energy cause major environmental problems that upset the fine balance of nature. The primary, as well as manufacturing industry sectors, are the major contributors to many of the environmental problems. Some of the ways in which development activities upset the fine balance of nature are outlined below.

### Changing Composition of the Atmosphere, Water, and Land

The composition of the atmosphere, water and land is by nature balanced.

However, pollution arising from development activities is disrupting this balance. Pollution is defined as direct or indirect alterations of the properties of the environment such as physical, thermal, biological or radioactive properties to create an actual or potential hazard to health, safety or welfare of any living organism.

The original sources of pollutants are the environmental resources, which form the **inputs.** Humans (society) use transformational tools (technology) to change the resources into consumable products. In the process, large concentrations of matter and energy are produced as bi-products (outputs). These may be in the form of solid wastes, particulate matter, and chemical wastes released into the three major sinks - air, water or land - causing air, water and land pollution.

We can now examine how pollution disrupts the natural balance of the atmosphere, water and land.

## Air Pollution

Some of the effects of air pollution include ozone layer depletion, acid rain, and the greenhouse effect.

## Ozone Layer Depletion

Ozone is a harmful pollutant at ground level which can damage plants, building materials, and human health. However, in the upper atmosphere (stratosphere), ozone is not a pollutant but it screens out dangerous ultraviolet rays from the sun at the surface of the Earth. Without this shield, all organisms would be subjected to the life-threatening radiation burns and genetic damage. A 1% loss of ozone results in about 2% increase in UV reaching the Earth's surface and could result in about one million extra human skin cancers per year worldwide if no protective measures are taken. Other health problems include cataracts of the eye, faster ageing of the skin, and weakened immune system. Crops also experience low yield due to UV interference with photosynthesis.

In 1985, the British Antarctic Atmospheric Survey announced the discovery of the "Ozone hole" over Antarctica. The hole was later found to cover 27.3 million $km^2$ in which all Ozone between 14kms and 20kms altitude was destroyed. Today, about 10% of all stratospheric Ozone worldwide has been destroyed. The destruction of the ozone layer is mainly caused by chlorine-containing molecules known as chlorofluorocarbons (CFCs) such as Freon 12($CCl_2F_2$ and halogen gases released into the atmosphere by humans. Chlorofluorocarbons (CFCs) are used as refrigerants and propellants in aerosol cans and as solvents and foam-blowing agents in the manufacture of plastic foams. CFCs were invented in

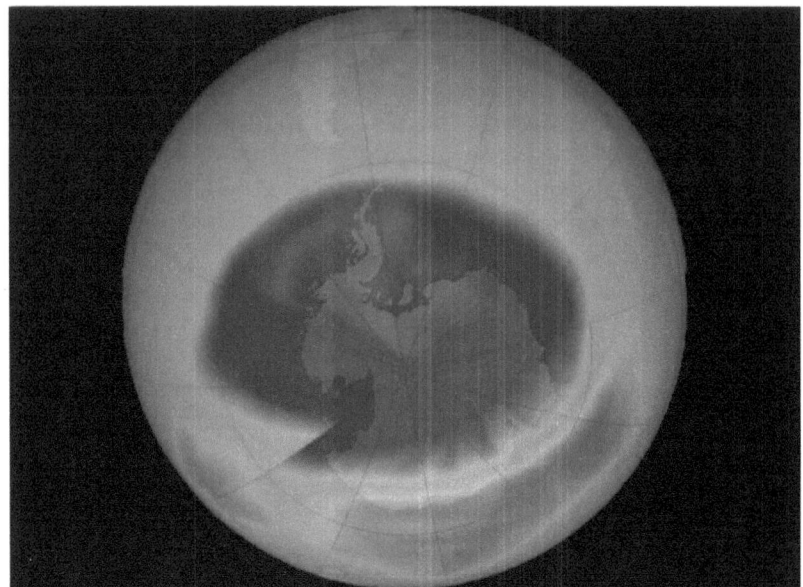

The ozone hole over Antarctica shrunk to its smallest maximum-extent in September 2017. Here, in this false-colour view of the monthly-averaged total ozone the blue and purple indicate areas with the least ozone, while yellows and reds mean the most ozone. Photo Caption/NASA

1928 by scientists at the American General Motors Company as a less toxic refrigerant.

Because their molecules are so stable, CFCs persist for a long time when released into the atmosphere. When they diffuse into the stratosphere, they are first broken down by ultraviolet light into reactive chlorine molecules in the form of chlorine monoxide thus destroying the ozone. Each of these molecules reacts with ozone molecules breaking them down. This is possible since the chlorine in CFCs catalyses the breakdown of ozone molecules and once in the stratosphere, the chlorine can remain there for a very long time. Since the chlorine molecules are themselves unaffected in the reactions, they continue to react with singlet oxygen atoms, also produced by UV radiation, thus continuing to destroy ozone for many years until they finally precipitate or are washed out of the air. As a result, the ozone layer depletion occurs which could allow dangerous solar radiation to reach the Earth's surface. It is estimated that by the year 2050, over 60% of the ozone layer will be gone.

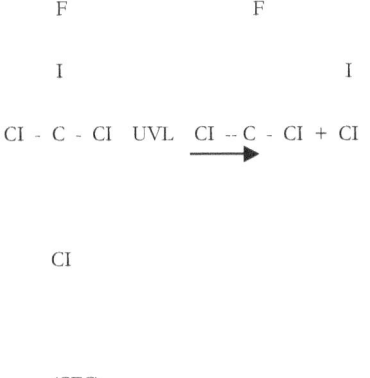

F                      F

I                         I

CI - C - CI  UVL  CI -- C - CI + CI

CI

(CFC)

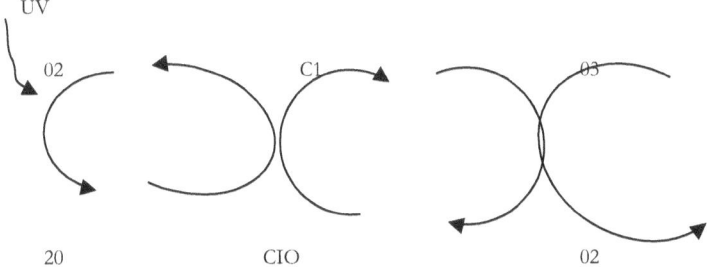

CFCs have measurably weakened the ozone layer. This will allow additional ultraviolet radiation to reach the surface of the Earth. Over Antarctica, weather patterns have enabled the CFCs to punch a huge seasonal hole of low ozone concentration in the ozone layer. Something similar is happening in the Arctic. This would increase skin cancer and cataract rates, depress immune systems and reduce crop yield throughout the world.

CFCs in the atmosphere takes about 75 years to release their chlorine, the continuous build-up of CFCs means that it is our children and grandchildren who will suffer most from its effects. International efforts through various agreements, such as the Montreal and Kyoto Protocols, have led to the reduction in the use of CFCs. Alternatives to CFCs for most uses already exist, such as hydrochlorofluorocarbons (HCFCs) which releases much less chlorine per molecule. In future, halogen free molecules may be used instead. CFC production in industrialised countries has fallen nearly 80% since the 1989 Helsinki Convention. Unfortunately, Ozone is a

The greenhouse effect occurs in nature when short-wavelength, high energy, solar radiation shines from the sun onto the surface of the Earth. Photo/CLIMATE CENTRAL

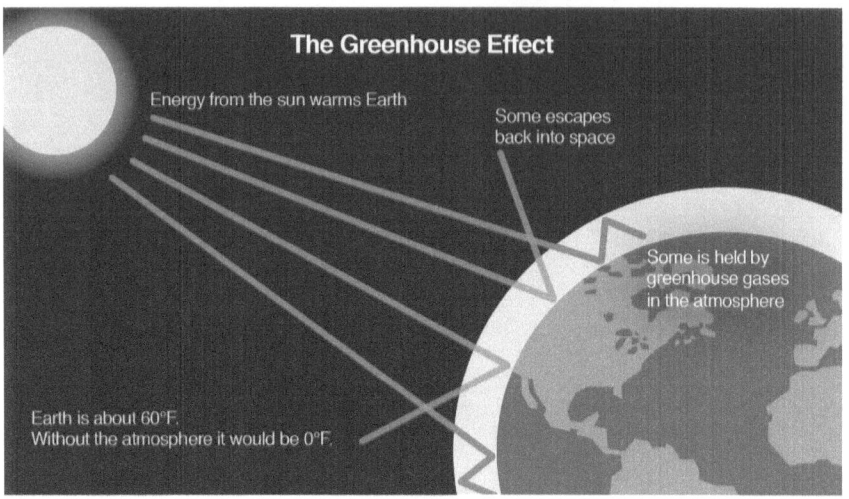

potent greenhouse gas and its reduction may accelerate global warming by offsetting the effects of increased carbon dioxide.

## Global Warming

Natural levels of carbon dioxide ($CO_2$) and other greenhouse gases in the atmosphere make life possible on Earth. Without them, the Earth would be a frozen desert. They act like glass in a greenhouse, letting the sun's rays through but trapping some of the heat in form of longwave radiation that would otherwise be radiated back into space. The **greenhouse effect** occurs in nature when short-wavelength, high energy, solar radiation shines from the sun onto the surface of the Earth. Some of this radiation is reflected by the atmosphere back into space. Some radiation passes through the atmosphere and is absorbed as it heats the air. About half reaches the Earth's surface. The Earth heats this up and in the process gives off longer – wavelength, lower energy infrared (heat) radiation. This infrared radiation passes into the atmosphere, but instead of being radiated, 100% goes back into space, much of it is absorbed by the atmosphere and re-radiated to the surface. This is due to many trace gases (greenhouse gases) in the atmosphere that is relatively transparent to the higher – energy sunlight, but traps or reflects the lower-energy infrared radiation. In this way, the Earth is warmed during the day. The Earth loses heat at night through outgoing infrared radiation. Over a lengthy period of time, because there is a balance between incoming and outgoing radiation, the Earth's temperatures remain constant.

Thus greenhouse gases act as a one-way filter, letting energy in the form of sunlight in but not allowing the infrared heat to escape at the same rate, and keeping the Earth's surface warm, maintained at a global average temperature of about 15°C. The Earth's surface would be a frozen mass if it were not for the natural greenhouse effect of the atmosphere. Without this phenomenon, the average global temperature would be in the order of - 17°C. It would actually be $33^0$ C colder than it is today. The Greenhouse gases that participate in this process include carbon dioxide, CFCs, methane, tropospheric ozone, nitrogen oxides, and water vapour.

Global warming is a result of the accelerated *greenhouse effect*. This is brought about by human intervention. Greenhouse gases are now accumulating very rapidly in the atmosphere, thus leading to the accelerated greenhouse effect. This is leading gradually to global warming. For example, the best-known greenhouse gas that contributes significantly to greenhouses gas is carbon dioxide. While a small effect, its concentration in the atmosphere has been increasing. It was approximately 250 ppm in 1850, 316 ppm in 1959 and 360ppm in 1959 and 360ppm in 1995. Its concentration is rising by about 0.5% annually due to increased burning of fossil fuels, deforestation and agriculture. Similarly, the level of methane (which is 30% more effective in trapping infrared radiation than $CO_2$) has been rising due to increased agricultural activities as are the levels of nitrous oxides. Today, about 22,000 million tons of $CO_2$ are emitted yearly (USA=4,800 million tons) in contrast to 320 million tons of methane (USA=50 million tons) and four million tons of nitrous oxide (USA=1.4 million tons) every year.

Recent human activity has led to a significant increase in the amount and type of greenhouse gases in the atmosphere, thus upsetting the natural balance. As more heat-absorbing gases accumulate in the atmosphere more solar radiation is trapped. This is preventing heat from escaping into space and is believed to be responsible for a rise in world temperatures which have risen by $0.5^0$ C this century. Estimates suggest that a further rise of between $1.5^0$ C and $4.5^0$ C could take place by the end of this century. The process by which world temperatures are rising is known as **global warming**. Carbon dioxide is the most important single factor (accounting for over 50% of effect) in global warming. It is produced by road transport and by burning fossil fuels in power stations, in factories and in the home. Since the industrialised countries consume 75% of the entire world's energy they are largely responsible for global warming. A secondary source of $CO_2$ is deforestation and the burning of the tropical rainforests. CFCs from aerosols, air conditioners, foam packaging, fire extinguishers and solvents for cleaning components of computers, and refrigerator coolants are the most damaging of the greenhouse gases and account for 25% of warming effect. Methane (10 %) released from decaying organic matter such as peat bogs, swamps, waste dumps, and animal dung, burning of fossil fuels and vegetation, bacterial action in the gut of ruminants and in the mud of rice paddies is also effective for greenhouse gas. Nitrous oxide

(5%) emitted from car exhausts, power stations and decomposition of agricultural fertiliser and animal wastes, in addition, contribute to the list of greenhouse gases.

The effects of global warming include the following:

- Sea temperatures will rise and sea-levels resulting from these will also rise by between 0.25 - 1.5 metres;
- Ice caps and glaciers, especially in polar areas will melt raising the level of the sea by another five metres. Even a rise of one metre could flood 25% of Bangladesh; and
- The distribution of precipitation will alter with some places becoming wetter and stormier, others becoming drier and with less reliable rainfall. For example, most parts of Sub-Sahara would become wetter than they are now while most equatorial regions would receive less rainfall than they do now.

What can be done about global warming?

$CO_2$ emissions can be reduced through various measures such as legislation against the level of emissions; use of electricity and other energy sources more efficiently; use of fuel in transportation more efficiently; use of solar energy; protection of forests and other vegetation and afforestation; improved agricultural practices; phasing out the use of CFCs; and saving all newspapers for recycling.

## Acid Rain

Some industrial wastes such as sulphur products are released into the atmosphere where they interfere with the water cycle by dissolving in rainwater to form **acid rain** which kills life and spoils roofs.

Acid rain has a pH value of less than 5 while pure water has a pH value of 7. Acid rain is caused by acid pollutants, mainly sulphur and nitrogenous compounds which make sulphuric and nitric acids when they dissolve in rainwater. The compounds are sulphur dioxide and nitrogen dioxide respectively. These are usually released into the atmosphere in great quantities from the burning of fossil fuels such as coal and oil in power plants, industrial boilers and car engines. They combine with water vapour, oxygen and sunlight in the atmosphere to create 'diluted acid soup'. A hydroxyl group is formed when a molecule of ozone breaks apart in the atmosphere, releasing oxygen atom which reacts with water. This is part of the photochemical reactions that occur in the atmosphere. The hydroxyl

Acid rain may cause extensive damage to materials and terrestrial ecosystems such as water, fish, vegetation, soils, and buildings. Photo/COURTESY

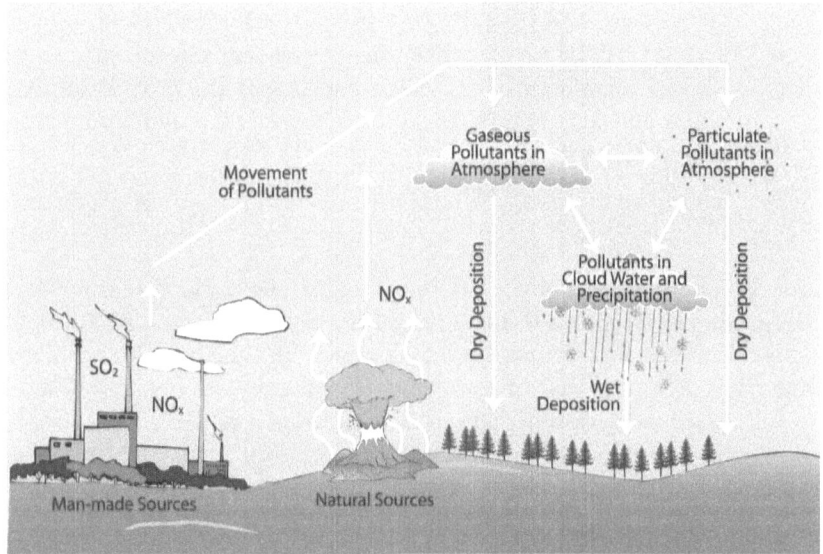

group is very reactive and starts the conversion of sulphur dioxide and nitrogen dioxide into sulphuric acid and nitric acid respectively. These gases are either carried by prevailing winds across seas and national frontiers to be deposited directly on to the Earth's surface (dry deposition) or are converted into acids which then fall to the ground in the snow or rain (wet deposition), thus polluting the air and causing untold damage to vegetation and buildings.

Acid rain phenomenon is common in the industrial countries in the Northern hemisphere. It was first noticed in Scandinavia in the 1950s when large numbers of freshwater fish died from acid poisoning deposited in the water by rain. Since then, the phenomenon has been prevalent in Western Europe and North America

Acid rain is responsible for many changes in the environment. For example, it:

- Corrodes various materials in buildings such as iron roofs;
- Renders water supplies more acidic;
- Causes increased the destruction of forests as important nutrients are washed away (leached), such as potassium and calcium and replaced by manganese and aluminium which are harmful to root growth. The trees become less resistant to drought, frost and disease over time;
- Dissolves calcium carbonate, which makes up a large part of cement, concrete and limestone from which many buildings are made thus corroding the buildings;
- Increases acidity of lakes and rivers thus killing fish and other

aquatic organisms when it lowers the pH of the water; and

- Increases acidity of soils thus affecting minerals in the soil, e.g. by releasing aluminium ions, which encourages the growth of some species and kills others; overall this reduces the number of crops that can be grown.

## Water Pollution

Water pollution is any physical, biological, or chemical change in water quality that adversely affects living organisms or makes water unsuitable for desired uses. Water pollution is a major source of human health problems. As much as 80% of all disease may be attributed to water contamination.

In terms of quantity, the major pollutants are silt and sediments from biomass production by aquatic organisms, land erosion and refuse discharge. The natural sources of water pollution are poison springs; oil seeps; Sedimentation from land erosion, runoff from croplands, grazing lands, and urban construction sites. The anthropogenic sources include factories, power plants, sewage treatment plants, underground coal mines, oil wells, runoff from farm fields and feedlots, golf courses, lawns and gardens, construction sites, logging areas, roads, streets and parking lots. All these pollutants make purification of water become expensive, hence, plants cannot carry out photosynthesis effectively as oxygen levels also decline. In some cases, they cause clogging of hydro-electric turbines.

The most serious water pollutants in terms of human health are pathogenic organisms from human and animal wastes. Pathogenic organisms (infectious agents) include bacteria, such as coliform (e.g. E.coli, salmonella); parasites, e.g. worms, filarial, trypanosome, Plasmodium; and viruses. These emanate from untreated or improperly treated human and animal wastes from sewage, feedlots, farm fields, food processing factories as well as untreated water. These organisms spread waterborne diseases such as typhoid, cholera, bacterial and amoebic dysentery, enteric fever and others such as polio, infectious hepatitis, and schistosomiasis. Diseases spread by insects that have aquatic larval – e.g. malaria, yellow fever, and filariasis.

Toxic organic chemicals (both natural and synthetic) used in the chemical industry to make pesticides pollute the water. This is mainly through improper disposal of industrial and household wastes containing dioxins, plastics, gasoline, pharmaceuticals, detergents, pigments used in everyday life. Runoff of pesticides from farms, forests, roadsides, golf courses, and other places where they are used in large quantities also contribute to pollution. In addition, organic wastes stored in dumps, landfills, lagoons and underground tanks may leak into surface water or groundwater or both. These may contribute to birth defects, genetic disorder, cancers, and disruption of ecosystems.

Toxic inorganic chemicals, such as acids, caustics, salts, and metals also pollute the water. Some are released from rocks by weathering or through mining, processing, using and discarding of minerals and carried by runoff into lakes, rivers or percolate into groundwater aquifers. Others are released from industrial effluents and household cleansers, including heavy metals that are highly toxic such as mercury, nickel, lead, tin, cadmium; super toxic elements such as selenium, arsenic; and high concentrations of salts, acids, nitrates and chlorine which are normally not toxic at low concentrations. These may all accumulate in food chains and have a cumulative effect on humans causing various disorders. Some may be neurotoxins. Salts affect plant growth in high concentrations and have poisoning effects in animals, such as birds. Acids and caustics cause corrosion of automobiles, and acidification of water and vegetation, thus reducing the level of organisms. They also facilitate leaching of soils, thus removing minerals into the water. Aluminium is the best example of this process.

Radioactive materials in minerals such as uranium, thorium, caesium, iodine, and radon from mining and processing of ores, power plants, weapons production as well as natural sources such as soils and rocks( especially through weathering, processing, using and discarding ) also contribute to pollution. They may cause mental disorders, nerve diseases and genetic disorders.

Water sources age fast due to sediments. In addition, oxygen-demanding wastes (animal manure, and plant residues) from sewage, agricultural runoff, paper mills, food processing factories, and tanneries reduce oxygen content (BOD) to less than 2 ppm thus supporting mainly anaerobic organisms and less of other organisms like fish and aquatic plants.

Thermal (heat) or raising or lowering water temperature due to electric power plants, metal smelters, petroleum refineries, paper mills, food processing factories, chemical industries that use and release cooling water may cause many problems. Discharge of heated water into water sources change water temperature thus affecting organisms such as corals. Water solubility levels are also affected thus affecting organisms negatively.

## Land Pollution

Humankind uses chemical fertilisers to increase crop productivity. However, 50% of these fertilisers used to benefit the crops, while the rest is lost from the soil by leaching, runoff and volatilisation. In addition, 90% of the pesticides used do not reach the target pests and contaminate the land (as well as water and air). Materials added to laundry detergents such as

Chemicals become more concentrated as they pass along the food chains and food webs.
Photo/PORTLAND HARBOR TRUSTEE COUNCIL

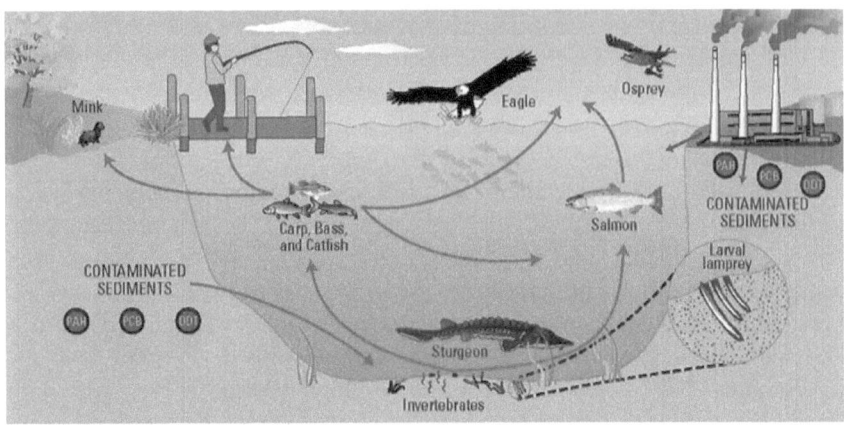

phosphates, nitrates, and a few other ingredients leach into the soil killing some organisms. In the same way, solid wastes, some hazardous, mainly from metallurgical, building and chemical factories pollute the land. Those which are non-biodegradable, remain in the soil for many years, producing chemicals containing barium, cadmium, chromium, manganese, nickel, silver and zinc most of which are harmful and may affect the health of plants and animals.

## Interference with Food Chains and Food Webs

The use of certain chemical products to improve the supply of goods and services to humankind inadvertently affects the fine balance of nature. The use of chemical compounds such as herbicides, fungicides, and insecticides kill pests and weeds but interfere with food chains and food webs. The chemicals become more concentrated as they pass along the food chains and food webs, thus persisting for a long time in the soil, rivers, lakes and bodies of animals, causing harm. For example, dichloro-diphenyl-trichloroethane (DDT) kills insects but some of it is taken in small quantities with food by animals and absorbed and stored in the body. As more DDT is absorbed, the quantity in the animal's body increases. If the animal is eaten by another animal or by a human being, the DDT from the dead animal passes into and remains in, the predator's body. As such, the higher up the food chain an animal is, the larger the amount of pesticide in its body. Birds of prey at the top of the food chain have been affected by DDT, like laying eggs with shells so thin that they easily break and few young birds survive.

Similarly, the use of chemical fertilisers to increase crop yield also interferes with the nitrogen cycle, as very little organic wastes remain in the soil. In addition, these together with some detergents such as powder soap containing phosphates and nitrates are dumped directly into streams, rivers and lakes, or are washed out of the soil by rain into these sinks, causing heavy growth of microscopic algae which block sunlight and oxygen from reaching other aquatic animals which then die thus, destabilising the aquatic ecosystems. This proliferation of the algae is referred to as algal bloom and it leads to eutrophication or enrichment of water bodies with nutrients. Plant nutrients (nitrates, phosphates, and ammonium) from agricultural and urban fertilisers, manure and sewage affect water clarity through eutrophication leading to increase in density of organisms and turbid or cloudy water with unpleasant taste and odour. In some cases, the level of nitrates getting into drinking water reaches dangerous levels particularly for babies and young children. Industrial effluents into rivers may also affect aquatic ecosystems and even people, particularly if the effluents contain poisonous waste products such as cyanide, arsenic and mercury.

## Changing Life Support Systems

Life support systems are the main ecosystems that moderate the essential ecological processes that keep the Earth fit for life. These include watersheds, wetlands, forests, coastal and freshwater systems, and soils. They shape climate, cleanse air and water, regulate water flow, recycle essential elements, create and regenerate soil and enable ecosystems to renew themselves. They are essential for food production, health and other aspects of human survival and sustainable development. However, human activities are permanently changing the life support systems in terms of their structure, function and diversity.

## Deforestation

Forests, for example, form a very important part of the life support systems of our environment. They (together with open woodlands) cover 40% of the Earth's land surface. They transform carbon dioxide to provide 25% of the earth's oxygen through photosynthesis. They are thus an important sink for carbon dioxide. They also maintain the water cycle, thus providing rainfall to vast regions of the earth. Forests moderate global climate by helping to stabilise the global temperatures and wind patterns by regulating the amount of solar radiation reaching the earth's surface. Forests also meet many people's basic, everyday needs, providing food, fuel, building materials, material for the manufacture of medicine and genetic resources and clean water. They are also home to millions of plant and animal species (biodiversity). The tropical rainforest is the richest and most complex ecosystems on the Earth's surface.

However, the forests are disappearing all over the world at a rate of over 20 million hectares per year through deforestation (for various development activities), desertification, and soil degradation. Before deforestation became intensive a few thousand years ago, rainforests covered about 14% of the Earth's surface. Today, they cover only about 7%. Much of this has been lost over the last 200 years with the coming of the industrial revolution. Tropical forests are fast contracting and almost half have been destroyed to allow for agriculture and settlement as well as providing timber. Africa's rainforests are being cleared at 4.1 million hectares each year while in the Amazon basin in South America where 20% of the rainforests have been cleared, the forest is disappearing at a rate of 14 hectares (14 football pitches) per minute. Half of the world's population depends on them for fuel, but about 100 million people in 22 countries no longer have enough trees to meet their minimal fuel needs. The forests are also removed to provide space for farming, settlement and construction of infrastructure such as roads. The forests also help to satisfy the needs of developed countries for the increasing demand for timber, especially hardwoods such as mahogany.

As forests are cut down, climatic balances are disrupted and fertile soils are washed away leading to desertification. This leads to many problems experienced in the world today, such as severe drought, soil erosion, floods, greenhouse effect and global warming. Global warming threatens to melt the polar ice caps and raise the sea levels, thus sub-merging coastal regions and islands. Moreover, deforestation leads to loss of biodiversity which co-exists with forests, such as birds, insects, reptiles and mammals. A typical patch of rainforest, $10km^2$, may contain as many as 1500 species of flowering plants, 400 species of bird, 750 species of tree, 150 varieties of butterfly, 100 different nutrient cycles and removal of canopy that facilitates soil erosion rendering soils heavily degraded. More significant, deforestation leads to interference with carbon and water cycles, and reduction in the amount of oxygen and water resources. It also leads to loss of cultural and social goods such as medicine for various societies who depend on the forests.

## Desertification

As forests are cut down, climatic balances are disrupted and fertile soil is washed away. The term 'desertification' is used when, on a historical timescale, land in arid and semi-arid regions (marginal land) is irreversibly degraded thus setting in desert-like conditions. The world's deserts are spreading and almost every continent is affected by desertification.

The main anthropogenic causes of desertification are over the cultivation of poor soils; overgrazing by animals on fragile rangelands; excessive cutting of fuelwood in drylands; deforestation, especially of upland watersheds; and inappropriate irrigation practices resulting in

The world's deserts are spreading and almost every continent is affected by desertification.
Photo/CARSTEN TEN BRINK/FLICKR

salinization or alkalisation of agricultural land. Droughts accelerate desertification and amplify its effects.

Desertification threatens about 35% of the world's land surface, affecting the lives of about 850 million people. Poor soil and harsh climates make animal husbandry or agriculture impossible without expensive imports of water, fertiliser, fodder and labour.

## Soil Degradation

About 30% of the Earth's surface is land, and only 11% of this is prime land for agriculture. Soil is a crucial life-support system consisting of vital nutrients, water, air and microorganisms that support the very existence of plant and animal life. Besides the bulk of all food production depends on it. In undisturbed ecosystems with a protective cover of plants, the soil is usually regenerated at the same rate it is removed. Nature takes 100 to 400 years or more to generate 10mm of topsoil, and 3,000 to 12,000 years would be needed to generate soil to a depth of 30 cm. Thus, it can take 1 to 4 centuries to produce 1cm of soil, and 30 to 120 centuries to produce a sufficient depth for farming. Once the soil has gone, it has gone for good. While the soil may thus be considered as a renewable resource, its ability to regenerate itself is therefore limited.

If soil and vegetation are not in balance, as often they are not when influenced by poorly managed human activities, erosion is accelerated with disastrous consequences. By the year 2000, one-third of the area that was ploughed in 1980 was reduced to dust. By 2020 another 30% could be lost.

An important aspect of soil loss is erosion. Thousands of millions of tonnes of soil are lost every year through soil erosion arising from deforestation and poor land management. Soil erosion is responsible for about 40% of land degradation worldwide. However, soil erosion is common in the tropics which are more susceptible to erosion than the temperate regions, due to the topography of the land and the nature of soils and rainfall. The tropics have extreme climatic conditions with seasonal and unreliable rainfall. Coupled with deforestation, there is usually no replacement of humus, no roots to bind the soil together, and the surface is left exposed to wind and rain. Whenever there is drought, winds blow away the soils. If rainfall occurs along with heavy thunderstorms and in sloppy areas, soils are washed downwards. In both cases, the land will be reduced to bare rock or left with deep, unusable gullies. More than half of India, for example, loses soil through erosion, floods, salinity and alkalinity. This loss is accompanied by the loss of nutrients, and habitats of beneficial organisms, leaving the land infertile.

## Change of the Carrying Capacity

There are finite limits to the carrying capacity of the Earth's ecosystems to the effects that they and the biosphere can withstand without permanent degradation. The Earth's carrying capacity must be supported by technologies that promote that capacity through prudent environmental management. In addition, avoidance of unnecessary consumption of resources and adoption of conservation methods that limit waste should be encouraged.

The use of renewable resources from ecosystems should be sustainable. These resources include soil, wild and domesticated organisms, forests, rangelands, cultivated land, and freshwater and marine ecosystems that support fisheries. A use is sustainable if it is within the resource's capacity for regeneration.

However, with varying levels of technology, humankind has tried to increase the carrying capacity of the land so that the ever-increasing population can receive the necessities of life, but in doing so, humans have been changing the carrying capacities of ecosystems unfavourably. For instance, through technology, humankind has been transferring water, soil, and air from one part of the earth to the other, thus reducing the amounts that existed somewhere else. In this way, man has been changing biosphere and thus upsetting the fine balance of nature.

Similarly, many animals and plant populations are threatened with extinction because human beings kill them for food, profit or sport. For example leopards, cheetahs, rhinoceroses, whales, crocodiles, elephants, turtles, tigers, and ostriches have been reduced to dangerously low levels through hunting in order to sell their skins and other parts. The blue whales have been reduced to about 6,000 down from a population of 2 million. The destruction of these resources affects the balance of ecosystems to which they belong apart from destroying the essential gene pools.

In addition, during farming, trees are felled, marshy areas are drained and the soil is ploughed up. These activities change the natural habitats and reduce the variety of plants and animals found there, thus changing the carrying capacity of the ecosystems permanently.

## Biodiversity Destruction

Biodiversity consists of living things and the ecosystems they inhabit and interact with. We can precisely say that biodiversity refers to the variety of life on Earth and to the natural patterns it forms. It includes all species of plants, animals and other organisms; the range of genetic stocks within each species, and the variety of ecosystems. Biodiversity, therefore, occurs at the genetic, species, ecosystem and landscape levels.

The extent of the world's species biodiversity is such that about two million of the estimated 10 - 15 million species have been scientifically identified. Specifically, around 1.2 million animals and 300,000 plants have been named or described by scientists. Millions more have yet to be identified. Biodiversity tends to be highest near the equator, where the solar radiation is strongest, and at sea level, where there is the least fluctuation in temperature.

Biodiversity provides goods such as foods and medicine and services such as clean water and air. It also guarantees the effective functioning of ecosystems and contributes to poverty reduction, food security, and human health (contributing to disease and illness prevention). However, the role of biodiversity in ecosystem functioning has not been fully determined.

Yet biodiversity is declining at an unprecedented rate. In addition **to five mass extinctions** in the distant past, the world is currently undergoing a sixth mass extinction. Most people are aware by now that many animal species are close to becoming extinct, but few seem to realise how severe the biodiversity crisis has become. This one has been caused by human activities. Research at the University of Florida indicates that during the last Ice Age, giant creatures were wiped out not by the change in climate, but by hunters. The sustainability of the forest ecosystems and other natural ecosystems are in danger from the expanding world population, which now totals more than six billion. With an estimated growth rate of 1.4% per year, it is projected to reach 12 billion by the year 2050. Further, due in large part to the growing human population and diverse human activities (supported in large part by fossil fuels), the current extinction rate of species ranges from approximately 1,000 to 10,000 times higher than natural extinction rates. This is alarming for several reasons.

Birds and mammals are becoming extinct at a very fast rate as are ecosystems such as coral reefs, freshwater wetlands and tropical rainforests. For example, in the last two or three decades, 20% of the world's freshwater fish have become extinct, threatened or endangered, while about 75% of the major marine fish stocks are either depleted, overexploited or being fished to capacity.

Human activities contribute to the loss of biodiversity. The continued decline in biodiversity is experienced through agricultural practices such as land clearance, habitat fragmentation and the introduction of pest species to terrestrial and marine ecosystems leading to a decline in genetic diversity. Habitat modification and destruction pose the greatest threat to biodiversity destruction. This is occasioned by the increase in human population necessitating increased demands for resources such as food, fuelwood, shelter, land and hence the need to convert habitats to other uses, such as settlement and agriculture. The development of urban areas and infrastructure and the draining and infilling of wetlands cause many species to become locked in ecological 'pockets' where they face extinction. Further losses are caused by changes in the food chain, the interruption of biological corridors needed for seasonal migrations, and the intrusion of alien species that dominate local ones. Indirect causes such as climate change may also contribute to extinctions.

The threatened ecosystems so far include:

- Tropical rainforests which have the greatest species biodiversity of any terrestrial ecosystem, and serve as sources of food, medicine, and fuel for surrounding communities. Nearly half of these forests have been cleared. As this is done many valuable species of animals and plants are threatened or lost forever;
- Wetlands which play an important role in water purification, waste filtration, and detoxification. They also stabilise soil and prevent erosion. More than half of the world's wetlands have been drained, leading to the extinction of about 50% of wetland species. The loss of wetlands leads to decreased water quality, and ability to absorb and hold precipitation thus leaving people vulnerable to natural disasters such as droughts, landslides, and floods. It also increases the chances of occurrence of waterborne diseases; and
- Coral reefs which are home to some of the earth's most diverse living ecosystems, fish and animals, are being destroyed through pollution, coastal development, fishing, tourism, siltation, and agriculture. Nearly 35% of the world's coral reefs have been destroyed or are threatened. The reefs usually provide income,

food and biomedical resources for coastal communities. They also act as a protection to shorelines from erosion, wave damage and storms.

The depletion of the gene pool has serious implications as about 40% of the global economy is based on biological products and processes. Loss of species also has a direct impact at the local level where the majority live in abject poverty and depend on direct use of biodiversity for food and livelihoods.

## Locking up important Elements

The depletion of non-renewable resources like minerals, oil, gas and coal must be minimised. While these cannot be used sustainably, their life can be extended, for example by recycling, by using less of a resource to make a particular product, or by switching to renewable substitutes where possible.

Production of non-biodegradable materials and wastes which lock important elements from returning to the natural cycles do not subscribe to this idea and commonly upset the natural balance. For example, materials such as furniture (steel and metal), polythene bags, plastic containers, synthetic fibres, iron and steel products do not easily decompose, neither are they easily dispensed with; hence, important elements contained in them are never released for recycling in natural environments.

## Depletion of Non-renewable Resources

These resources cannot regenerate themselves. They include minerals, oil, gas, and coal. While these cannot be used sustainably, their 'life' can be extended, for example by recycling, using less of a resource to make a particular product, or by switching to renewable substitutes where possible. These practices are essential if the Earth is to sustain billions of more people in future and give everyone a life of decent quality.

## Increased Consumption of Renewable Resources as measured by Ecological Footprint

The consumption of renewable, like that of non-renewable resources, has continued to sour as population increases and as a population becomes more affluent. While these resources may be regenerated but their use should not be well beyond the rate at which the planet earth replenishes the resources.

Ecological Footprint (EFP) is one way of determining the consumption of renewable resources by the various groups of people, schools, countries or the world. This is done by converting the resources into acreage and calculating this against the population.

According to the Ecological Footprint of Nations (2004), the average African was less than 1.4 hectares per person in 1999, the average Australian footprint was close to 7.1 hectares, while that of the average American was 9.6 hectares per person. The EFP for the average world consumer was 2.3 hectares per person or 20% above the earth's biological capacity of 1.9 hectares per person. This means that humanity now exceeds the planet's capacity to sustain its consumption of renewable resources.

---

## Box 3.1

### Discussion

Do you now notice that the greatest challenge we face today is to bring about changes in the living conditions of our people while safeguarding the environment for future generations? This can be achieved through informed development activities in which the economic and social conditions of the people are improved without damaging the natural resources on which they depend. This kind of development is referred to as **sustainable development**.

---

## Summary

Development is defined as the modification of the biosphere and the application of human, financial, living and non-living resources to satisfy human needs and improve the quality of human life. Development is needed for several reasons such as to meet the basic needs of humanity, such as food, clothing, shelter and source of livelihoods (jobs); to improve the quality of life for humanity in terms of literacy, life expectancy, nutrition, health, sanitation, clean water among others; and to provide energy which is an essential need. In an effort to meet these needs and aspirations, nations rely on their resource base. These resources are transformed into goods and services needed in satisfying the human needs and aspirations. The extent to which this is achieved depends on the level of energy consumption and industrialisation.

The developed countries with a high level of industrialisation can easily meet these needs as compared with developing countries which face immense challenges against industrialisation due to low levels of technology, lack of adequate non-renewable resources, lack of adequate energy resources, social organisation, and the ability of the biosphere to absorb the effects of industrialisation.

However, development is considered as a necessary evil. It has led to untold destruction of the environment in terms of pollution, depletion of the resource base, extinction of species, soil erosion, climate change, among others. The greatest challenge we face today is to bring about changes in the living conditions of our people while safeguarding the environment for future generations. This can be achieved through informed development activities in which the economic and social conditions of the people are improved without damaging the natural resources on which they depend. This kind of development is referred to as **sustainable development**.

## End of Chapter Activities

- What do you understand by the terms development, economic development, economic growth, and sustainable development?
- Discuss the advantages and disadvantages of development.
- Explain how sustainable development could make the process of development more useful.

## Bibliography

Ecological Footprint of Nations (2004),
        http//www.redifiningprogrss.org/publications/footprintnations2004.pdf

United Nations (2002),
        United Nations Report of the World Summit on Sustainable Development, Johannesburg, 26 August-4 September 2002.New York: United Nations(http://www.johannesburgsummit.org/html/documents/summit.docs/131302-wssd-report-reissued.pdf.

# 4

# CHAPTER 4

# ENVIRONMENTAL CRISIS

## Introduction

In the previous chapter, you were introduced to the nature of the natural environment provided by the planet Earth and how this has been utilised for the purpose of development. You have learned that all components of the environment occur in a balanced manner but if this balance is interfered with the consequences are likely to be dire. In this chapter, you will learn about the role of humankind in the stability of ecosystems. You will examine the ways in which human societies have impacted on the quality of the environment leading to a situation commonly referred to as the environmental crisis.

**Expected Learning Outcomes**

By the end of this topic you should be able to:

- Demonstrate the ability to define the term environmental crisis;
- Outline and discuss the various categories of environmental crises;
- Analyse critically the historical roots of the environmental crisis; and

- Discuss the major human factors responsible for the environmental crisis we experience today.

## Meaning of Environmental Crisis

Since 1960, major environmental problems have been identified which affect the global environment. There is evidence of a progressive loss of ecological stability where indicators include shrinking of forests, expansion of deserts, loss of cropland, increase in pollution, and an increase in poverty levels. These environmental problems afflicting the Earth's environment have taken a long period of time to build up. Collectively, they contribute to the phenomenon referred to as the 'environmental crisis' that we are currently experiencing. Before we outline some of these environmental problems, it is necessary to first discuss what environmental crisis is all about.

The environmental crisis is a situation in the environment demanding immediate corrective action to avert further deterioration, damage or destruction of the affected environment. However, people's perceptions of environmental crisis differ. An environmental crisis may be considered in terms of local, national and global levels. Not all may agree that a given circumstance constitutes a crisis. Nevertheless, since 1962, when Rachel Carson wrote her book *'Silent Spring'* many voices have been raised in alarm over the degraded state of the global environment. Responses to the alarm varying substantially, some people say the cries are exaggerated, others say they are genuine.

An example of a local crisis is the water hyacinth menace in Lake Victoria which upsets the ecological balance of the affected parts of the lake. It also greatly affects the day-to-day social and economic activities of the people who depend on the lake for their livelihood. These observations are severe enough to merit being referred to as a crisis. But because the observations do not immediately and directly affect or threaten other people in the country or the world, the crisis is thus local and may go unnoticed by the larger community.

On the other hand, the diminishing supply of energy in Kenya, both wood fuel and electricity, due to increased demand, affects the whole country, hence referred to as a national crisis. The problem is manifested in increased deforestation and frequent power failures in the country. The energy crisis due to the diminishing supply of fossil energy since the 1970s constitutes a global environmental crisis and merits attention by the whole world community.

The environmental crisis is thus a phenomenon covering the Earth's environment ranging from local to global levels. The threat of the crisis may range in magnitude from deterioration of small ecosystems to

The water hyacinth in Lake Victoria, Kenya. Photo/MICHELL ZAPPA/FLICKR

total destruction of the biosphere. However, there is no general agreement on whether and when the world as a whole will face a crisis or crises. But the Brundtland Report observes that any disruption of the photosynthetic process through accelerated deforestation, pollution, climate change or ozone layer depletion could lead to a definite global environmental crisis. This is because all life depends on this process in terms of the availability of oxygen and food and other resources through primary production. Given that at present we are using about 40% of the total primary production of photosynthesis in one generation, when population doubles, humankind will use 80% of the primary production. Even if climate change and pollution do not drastically impair photosynthesis, the limits to sustainable production are being reached. Within two generations a crisis seems likely unless the population slows or primary production can be highly improved.

## Categories of Environmental Crises

Since the 1960s when Rachel Carson wrote her book *Silent Spring*, the following major global environmental problems can be identified:

- **Climate change**: Due to accelerated global warming and Greenhouse effect. It affects the photosynthetic process directly;
- **Soil degradation**: Through the loss of productive land through

erosion. Primary productivity will decline;

- **Deforestation:** Due to loss of tropical rainforest. This leads to global warming, hence climate change;
- **Loss of biodiversity:** Due to the extinction of flora and fauna. Loss of biodiversity- through –deforestation, overfishing, exposure of the coast to storms and erosion and pollution. This leads to Genetic erosion;
- **Population increase**: Leads to over-exploitation of resources;
- **Economic stagnation or depression**: If an economy fails to grow over a long period of time, it experiences stagnation and leads to Depression and inflation thus increasing level of poverty;
- **Ozone layer depletion**: Due to the release of CFCs (chlorofluorocarbons) in the atmosphere;
- **Agrochemical Pollution**: Particularly from use of pesticides and fertilisers;
- **Pollution of the land**: Due to the dumping of solid wastes. Dumping of industrial wastes is a very dangerous practice that is accelerated due to the lack of stringent laws and regulations on the dumping of wastes. Nuclear waste disposal accident can be very catastrophic. Chernobyl disaster explosion of a nuclear plant- led to radiation emissions - very dangerous;
- **Depletion of natural resources**: Consumerism - People wanting always to eat and buy things. Industries need to expand on their productivity hence more resources are used and a lot of wastes are disposed of. Depletion of freshwater resources - the amount of fresh water globally is 1% of all the water masses. Agro-chemical pollution - pesticides, herbicides, fungicides, and insecticides. This is common in large-scale agricultural producing countries like China, Argentina and Brazil;
- **Eco-refugees**: These are refugees, who come as a result of ecological problems e.g. droughts, floods, and tsunami etc.;
- **Acid rain**: Common in temperate regions (northern hemisphere) due to high levels of industrialisation - chemical wastes dissolve in the rain making chemical rain;
- **Terminal diseases**: Such as HIV / AIDS and cancer; and
- **Technology**: Particularly inappropriate technology is devastating to a country. Biotechnology used to produce food in large amounts; of different variations but if it is misused e.g. cloning which becomes a threat. Genetic engineering accidents e.g. escape or uncontrolled release of harmful biological agents.

These problems can be further put into the following **four categories** of perceived or potential crisis at local, national and global levels:

- Category 1: Greatest Risk and Increasing Threat
- Category 2: Medium Risk
- Category 3: Least Risk
- Category 4: Threats

Category 1: Crises Pausing Greatest Risk and Increasing Threat

These are both at national and global levels:

- Climate change due to accelerated global warming;
- Soil degradation through the loss of productive land through soil erosion;
- Deforestation due to loss of tropical rain forests;
- Greenhouse effect leading to global warming and climate change;
- Genetic erosion due to the extinction of flora and loss of biodiversity;
- Population increase that leads to overexploitation of resources; and
- Toxic releases via effluents, accidents, warfare and agrochemicals.

Category 2: Crises Pausing Medium Risk (at national and global Levels)

- Economic stagnation and depression;
- Ozone layer depletion;
- Agro-chemical pollution due to the use of pesticides;
- Dumping of industrial wastes; and
- Consumerism, leading to over-exploitation of resources and disposal of wastes.

Category 3: Crises Pausing Least Risk (at the global level)

- CFCS – Leading to the destruction of the ozone layer

Category 4: Threats (at national and global levels)

- Biological warfare – use of biological resources for killing people;
- Depletion of freshwater resources;
- Genetic engineering accidents – escape or uncontrolled release of

harmful biological agents;

- Eco-refugees to due ecological problems;
- Nuclear warfare;
- Nuclear accident and waste disposal e.g. Chernobyl disaster explosion of nuclear plant;
- Agro-chemical pollution – pesticides, herbicides, fungicides, and insecticides;
- Acid rain;
- Chemical warfare;
- Loss of biodiversity through deforestation, overfishing, pollution, and erosion;
- Biotechnology misuse – e.g. cloning;
- HIV/AIDS; and
- Inappropriate technology.

## Historical Roots of Environmental Crisis

The planet Earth has gone through various periods of dramatic change as a result of the interaction of human culture and the natural environment. Such a change is referred to as a *revolution*.

Revolutions have often changed the Earth's environment, culminating in the present environmental crises. The revolutions that have had dramatic effects on the global environment are an agricultural revolution; civilisation; industrial revolution; and modernisation or technological revolution.

Prior to these revolutions, societies had not begun. Our ancestors lived by gathering fruits and seeds of wild plants and by hunting wild animals. There were no permanent settlements because small groups of people were constantly in search of food and shelter. Our ancestors had little control over their environment. Therefore, they did not clear the forests to grow crops and build houses and they did not interfere with the harmony of the ecosystems.

### Agricultural revolution

The agricultural revolution began about 11,000 years ago in Mesopotamia and later in China and Egypt. The revolution started when man in Mesopotamia learnt to plant the seeds of wild wheat. This was necessary because the domesticated variety could no longer reproduce itself naturally. Without civilisation, it could soon die out and become extinct. Later, they learnt to grow other crops and settle in one place. Thus, people developed a new culture namely farming which was carried out in large locations. They used fairly simple tools made of stones and iron ore to till the land and to clear the forests. As this culture continued to spread over the communities the number of people dependant on hunting and gathering declined.

At the same time or a little later, domestication of animals such as dogs, sheep, goats and cattle began. Since that time, a few more animals have been domesticated. Today, more of the world's people are engaged in agriculture than in any other occupation.

The culture of farming brought about several changes in the environment then.

a) Soil erosion

The clearance of vegetation for agricultural purposes and for settlement left the soil bare and it was easily washed away whenever it rained. This progressively rendered the soil less fertile.

b) Desertification

Many areas where the agricultural revolution began such as Iraq, Iran, Egypt, Libya, Saudi Arabia and parts of China are now deserts. These areas are believed to have been originally grasslands and forests. Domestication of animals and arable farming most probably led to the process of desertification through a gradual loss of vegetation.

c) Destabilisation of ecosystems

As the people continued clearance of vegetation for farming and settlement there was interference with the return of minerals to the ecosystems. Similarly, minerals that were absorbed by crops were not allowed to return to the soil after harvesting. This began the process of upsetting the nutrient balance.

d) Biodiversity Destruction

The farming activities brought about the loss of original gene pools of wild grains which became extinct. This happened because of a gene selection through monoculture, hybridisation and selection of plant varieties for propagation while clearing others. Many other species of plants and animals became extinct as well since they never adapted to the new natural habitats created through clearance of vegetation. This was the beginning of biodiversity destruction.

## Civilisation

Civilisation began about 6,000 years ago in the fertile river valleys of Tigris and Euphrates (Mesopotamia), the Nile (Egypt), Hwang Ho and Si Kiang

(China), and the Hindus and Ganges (India). Civilisation grew from the agricultural revolution. First, the expansion of agriculture by using ploughs and through irrigation led to greater harvests of crops. With increased food, the human population also increased, as was the number of families and villages. This necessitated the establishment of central governments and people began to live as societies under common laws. Such laws were necessary to preserve people's way of life and to prevent chaos; thus civilisation had begun.

Eventually, the powerful cultures or civilisations extended their influence to their neighbours. The civilisation developed unique culture as expressed in their architecture, writing, arts and other artefacts, such as weapons and tools. They used environmental resources in developing these materials. The heat energy required for domestic use and for making tools and weapons was derived from burning wood, cow dung and charcoal. Later, they learnt to use running water to drive wheels, to raise water for irrigation and to grind grain. The wind was also used to power boats and drive windmills, which raised water from the wells and pumped it into the fields. Civilisation lasted for several thousands of years reaching its peak in the 15th and 17th centuries during which the greatest geographical discoveries and the opening of nearly all territories of the terrestrial surface were experienced. This also coincided with the development of tools and means of production and the formation of large cultural economic centres. This success encouraged the extraction and exploitation of many natural resources. Radical changes in ecological systems started taking place on a large scale.

Some of the consequences of civilisation include the following:

a) Depletion of resources

Increased population in civilisation areas, led to increased use of natural resources particular metal ores and wood leading to early depletion of this resources.

b) Pollution

Heat energy for looking and making tools and weapons was derived from burning wood, charcoal and cow dung. This began the process of air pollution.

c) Soil degradation

The hydraulic technology used to raise water from wells and rivers for irrigation or for grinding grain facilitated salinisation of the soils and silting of rivers and irrigation channels. The invention of plough also led to an increase in the area of tilled land and turned to the diminishing fertility of the soil. The initial stage of soil degradation had begun.

### d) Deforestation

Increased use of wood to provide the source of heat energy and for building led to deforestation this probably contributed to desertification in the areas surrounding the Nile, Tigris, Hwang Ho and Si Kiang valleys.

## Industrial Revolution

The industrial revolution started a little over 200 years ago, in Great Britain and the countries around the North Sea in Europe. The industrial revolution was a series of events and inventions that utilised scientific ideas. Specifically, it started when James Watt invented the steam engine on January 5th, 1769.

Machines were gradually invented which used a new source of energy such as steam. This eventually replaced muscle power, wind and falling water in providing power to do work. Wood fuel was burnt to boil water thus proving steam. Later, new forms of energy were discovered and used, particularly fossils fuel such as coal, gas and oil.

The revolution was therefore characterised by changes in the means of production and by the transition from manufactory to large-scale machine industry. The revolution created the greatest changes and crises in the environment that we experience today. With the diversification of energy resources and with the discovery of minerals such as iron, coal, oil, copper, aluminium and several others many products such as tools, weapons, cutlery, ships and bridges, were manufactured which found readily available markets. The resources that were scarce were imported from colonies in Africa, Asia and Latin America. Hence, resources from these continents contributed immensely to the industrial revolution. The prevailing economic system at the time was capitalism. The major aim of economic ventures was to create and accumulate wealth and profits. The safety of the environment did not matter. The period was characterised by profound consumption of environmental resources to satisfy human needs and wants.

The consequences of the industrial revolution were as follows:

### a) Deforestation

Enormous amounts of forests were cut down in Western Europe and in the colonies for the purpose of providing wood fuel. England, for instance, does not have the original forest cover. This process of deforestation began the process of the Greenhouse effect and Global warming being experienced today.

b) Biodiversity destruction

The destruction of habitats due to the mining of coal, iron and other minerals and due to deforestation, led to the extinction of many important species, of plants and animals in Europe and even in Africa, Latin America and Asia. This also led to the beginning of the destruction of genetic resources.

c) Depletion of Resources

The industrial revolution sharply increased the exploitation of natural resources and finite energy resources begun to be exploited particularly wood, coal and oil. Colonies were formed from where some of the raw materials could be obtained cheaply and this process continues up to now in different forms. For example, importation of very unique trees in the Congo forest is drastically leading to the depletion of the tropical forest and important genetic resources.

d) Pollution

The increased exploitation of natural resources for industrial production changed man's influence upon ecosystems. The factories began emitting chemical fumes and effluents into the environment and intensified the initial stage of air, soil and river contamination. For example, London became one of the most polluted cities in Europe darkened with coal smoke. Many people died of lung diseases from this pollution. The level of $CO_2$ in the global atmosphere started to increase sharply since 1850, thus beginning the process of the accelerated greenhouse effect.

e) Cultural miscegenation or pollution

The rapid switch from agriculture to manufacturing was painful. People were evicted from rural areas to towns where life was miserable. Overcrowding, crime and pollution brought misery and cultural confusion among people. Child labour became rampant. Community values started to vanish. New values were created throughout Western Europe which was referred to as Western civilisation or culture. We are all grappling with the culture today.

## Technological Revolution

As a result of the Industrial Revolution, modernisation began in Europe in the twentieth century. It is primarily the application of advanced technology to production thus making it more efficient. It is also referred to as the Technological Revolution.

Modernisation was characterised by the introduction of an entirely new process of new materials and energy production by a qualitative leap in the means of production and the industrial output of new items with diverse technological, economic, physical and chemical properties. It spread from Europe to other parts of the world at varying rates depending on how accessible that part was from Europe.

In some places in the world, the ideas were eagerly adopted. In others, it was resisted. Today, largely as a result of the modernisation the world can be divided into three basic types of societies:

- Modern Industrial societies or Developed world or The North or the First world;
- Traditional and chiefly agricultural societies or Developing world or The South or Third world countries; and
- Transitional societies or Newly Industrialized societies or Second world societies of South East Asia, Malaysia, Philippines, Indonesia.

Technological revolution or modernisation has only helped to prolong the effects of development on the environment that began in the Industrial Revolution. This has resulted in the destruction of forests leading to accelerated deforestation, soil erosion and climatic change; destruction of biodiversity; depletion of natural resources such as coal, gas, oil, arable land and several others; and pollution of the atmosphere; and diminishing of freshwater resources.

## The Root Causes of Environmental Crisis

There are several explanations for the ecological crisis that we are experiencing today. These explanations include, but are not limited to: humankind's perception about the environment and the manner of interaction with the environment; the level of technology; poverty; ignorance; increased population; and policies of economic production and property ownership.

### Perception of Environment

Humankind's use of resources depends on the way they perceive the environment and its resource base. For a long time, human perception with regard to environmental resources has been guided by two broad philosophies of Anthropocentricism and Environmentalism.

This is the belief that humankind and environment are two separate entities and that the environment is meant to subordinate the needs and wants of humankind. This is sometimes referred to as purpose ethic. Humankind has dominion over a world whose parts and inhabitants exist solely for the benefit of and welfare of humankind. This has led to the extinction of many species.

The philosophy is averse to interdependence and integration of people with the environment. If your environment is poor then you are doomed; if it is rich then you exploit it to your own advantage. Nature exists for the satisfaction of human wants and needs.

The paradigm consists of a range of beliefs such as Environmental determinism (that the environment determines the fate of society); possibilism (that man is able to do virtually anything despite environment); probabilism (that certain advanced cultures can overcome the constraints of the environment); and romanticism. However, determinism was more dominant.

This philosophy was rampant during the industrial revolution and reached its peak between 1914 – 1945 when colonialism and the second world wars were experienced. Indeed, the Europeans pioneered it in the industrialisation of society and hence set in motion the process of environmental degradation.

The philosophy in part explains the causes of the two world wars as summarised in this statement: "*He who rules the heartland (Germany) rules Europe he who rules Europe rules the world.*" The Germans had superior and abundant resources both natural and human and began building war planes, automobiles, with which they used to engage the rest of Europe in war.

The major factor that seems to have encouraged the Europeans to begin the industrial revolution is the Judaeo-Christian tradition peculiar to Western Europe Christianity. This tradition finds its strength in the Biblical faith as illustrated in the book of Genesis chapter 1:27-30. It is believed that this view has from the Roman times influenced how people in the West perceived the environment and it is largely to blame for the present world environment and development predicament

Colonialism in Kenya. Colonialism in Africa was established to collect raw materials for the growth of the western states. Photo/COURTESY

The tradition has tended to separate humankind from the natural environment. He has been given dominion and may investigate and appropriate the objects of nature without reference to anybody else. These were the beliefs that guided the industrial revolution as expressed in the writings of the early scientists like Francis Bacon in the Seventeenth and Eighteenth centuries.

The philosophy emanates from the founders of the scientific revolution like Francis Bacon (1561 – 1626), Rene Descartes (1596 – 1650) and Isaac Newton (1642 – 1727). They believed that science and technology should be used to dominate and control nature. Nature was viewed as a material resource to be exploited for productive progress. Since the industrial revolution humankind has therefore exploited resources indiscriminately as if this did not have a long term effect on himself.

Even the relationship between Europeans and Africans has been along with a similar exploitative relationship. The colonies were established in Africa mainly to provide raw materials for the then fast expanding factories in Europe and as markets for the finished products. Africans in these colonies were regarded by Europeans as being of low mental capacity, having been impaired by the hostile tropical climate. They believed that the best thing for the Africans was to be slaves. This perception was largely deterministic.

Presently, the computer revolution has hastened resource exploitation. Every state is striving to employ the power of the computer to attain rapid economic growth. More and more resources are being used to produce consumer goods at the expense of resources conservation. This model of economic growth is deterministic, too, and is causing rapid environmental degradation. Commitment to the anthropocentric perspective of the environment (that nature exists for satisfying human needs and wants) has produced a progressive deterioration in environmental quality.

The key features of this philosophy are as follows:

- The technological man has lost contact with environments that sustain civilisation;
- That we should increase the human population at will since the environment is still virgin. This leads to the destruction of the environment faster than expected;
- All types of environments must be conquered for human exploitation – no environment should remain virgin;
- The environmental resources are infinite and must the, therefore, be exploited fully (*Superabundance Ethic*). This is a fallacy as all parts of the environment are limited – air, water, sunlight;
- The atmosphere and the waters of the earth can absorb unlimited quantities of pollutants by dilution. This is erroneous as pollution has drastically reduced the quality of the atmosphere, land and water;
- Progress is equated with a change toward improvement. However, change is progress when an environmental condition has been improved, not worsened; and
- In terms of land, water and other resources, man aspires to own them all. But should we still have absolute property ownership in the hands of a few people? Land sharing, land trusteeship may be necessary to safeguard the rights of all members of society.

## Environmentalism

This philosophy challenges the validity of Anthropocentricism. It is concerned with finding new forms of co-existence with nature. Nature should not be exploited for the benefit of man alone, it should also be preserved for its own sake and for posterity.

Whereas this may be a new phenomenon in Western cultures, it was and still is prevalent in the traditional societies of the world such as the original inhabitants of Australia (Aborigines), New Zealand (Maoris) and the Red Indians of South America as well as among the African cultures. These communities were, and to some extent are, more sympathetic to nature than their European counterparts. For them, there is no distinction between God and the environment. But even among these communities, things are changing.

Most traditional African societies had a deep knowledge and understanding of the ecosystems they inhabited. They had learned to live in harmony with the environment. They achieved this goal by observing a myriad of customary laws and taboos. For them, life and Earth were inseparable. They saw the Earth as a source of spirituality, the fountain from which culture and language flourished. It is the provider of food, medicine, clothing and protection, the mother of our race. This was the case of traditional environmentalism. Poritt says:

> *Whereas industrial nations exploit and destroy, tribal peoples, nurture and manage their varied habitats in subtle and efficient ways that have stood the test of millennia… (save the Earth).*

Some of the traditional societies known for traditional environmentalism include the Bukusu (Luhyia) of Western Kenya who valued three wetland ecosystems:

- Special places where livestock obtain water and minerals from a special mixture (Esilongo);
- Special places where mud is obtained to decorate candidates for initiation (circumcision); and
- Special places where secondary initiation rites are performed (Esitabichia).

To protect these ecosystems, these places were declared sacred. These were often also sources of water and were water catchment areas. Rare species and varieties of plants and animals were also protected through taboos. When the Europeans came to Africa they believed that African customs and religions were backward and their language inferior. Little did the Africans know that the Europeans were coming with a lifestyle that negated the very survival of their ecosystems. The African cultural values that aided in conserving their ecosystems are now at crossroads.

Modern Environmentalism, as enshrined in the principles and ideals for Environmental Education, is now reaching the hearts of the all the people across the world largely through the work of the United Nations and its agencies such as UNEP, UNESCO, IEEP and many NGOs. The goal is to leave behind a minimally degraded environment for future generations. Modern Environmentalism consists of two major opinions i.e. Biocentrism and the New Environmental Paradigm.

Biocentrism has three related perspectives that shape this position i.e. Gaia Hypothesis, Deep Ecology and Radical Environmentalism. According to this view, people should endeavour to conserve the environment even at the cost of inflicting some hardships on humankind.

The New Environmental Paradigm advocates for sustainable use of environmental resources so that both the environment and mankind benefit from the mutual interaction. Some of the key features of this philosophy are as follows:

- The quest for environmental quality will never become a reality until a new environmental ethic replaces the out-dated one;
- People should have reverence for all life;
- People should respect the right of existence for all environments; and
- People should accord the highest priority to environmental quality.

**Box 4.1**

### Discussion

Do you know that since the time environmental education began following the various United Nations mediated conferences up to Rio de Janeiro and Johannesburg conferences, little had practically happened in terms of environmental improvement?. We still experienced more destruction of the environment, pollution, human greed, poverty, disease, and corruption. There has been unprecedented environmental awareness, but people don't walk the talk. There has been a Nature Deficit Disaster (NDD), resulting in the environmental crisis.

Clearly, the root causes of the environmental crisis include:

- Human greed (consumerism);
- Media advertisements glorifying consumerism;
- Multi-national companies;
- Lack of altruism;
- Poverty;
- Negative attitudes;
- Population growth;

- Ignorance;
- Resistance to change; and
- Power relationships such as the gap between the rich and the poor countries

## Summary

In this chapter, you have learned about the human factor in the Earth's environmental crisis. This involved an understanding of the meaning of environmental crisis and the various environmental problems that constitute the different dimensions of the environmental crisis. You learned that environmental crisis implies that the environment is deeply affected but it can be salvaged if corrective measures are taken in good time. You observed that the Earth's environmental problems result in crises that may be at local, national, regional or global levels.

You also learned that the environmental problems we experience today are a result of many years of human interaction with the environment. The magnitude of the problems depends on the level of social organization and the technological advancement of society. The interactions by earlier societies did not quite impact on the environment as those societies which lived in the era of the industrial revolution and modern times.

It became apparent to you that western civilisation where the industrial revolution began valued the application of science to develop technology with which environmental resources were transformed into usable products. This resulted in more drastic environmental changes as compared to the traditional societies in Africa and Asia that used indigenous knowledge and rudimentary technologies to make basic needs such as clothing and shelter.

Finally, you learned about the root cause of the environmental crisis we experience today. It was seen that the biblical teachings seemed to influence the human perceptions of the need to exploit the environment through applications of science and technology. This seems to influence the emergence of the industrial and the technological revolutions, and therefore the decline of environmental quality. Western European societies, therefore, exhibited a deterministic view of the environment. The indigenous societies did not seem to be influenced by these perceptions and continued to interact with their environments in a sustainable manner. They exhibited traditional environmentalism. However, many of these societies are also now being influenced by western civilisation and are drastically changing their environments as well. These tendencies have attracted the need to introduce environmental education or modern environmentalism in an effort to mitigate the senseless degradation of the global environment.

## End of Chapter Activities

- What do you understand by the term environmental crisis?
- One author recently said '-------there is no general agreement on whether and when the world will face an environmental crisis or crises'. Provide any five reasons to support this statement.
- Using relevant examples, distinguish between determinism and environmentalism as they relate to the environmental crisis we experience today.
- Outline any five consequences of the industrial revolution.
- Give any five key features of the civilisation era.
- With reference to one ethnic group in Kenya known to you outline how the group conserved the environment.

## Bibliography

Cunningham, W.P, Cunningham M.A and Saigo, B.W (2003)
    Environmental Science: A Global Concern. McGraw-Hill.
Korir- Koech (1988)
    Environmental Education PAC 101 Faculty of External Degree
    Studies, University of Nairobi.
Muyanda-Mutebi, P(Ed)
    Environmental Education: A Teaching and Training Guide Pan
    Africa Books.
Muthoka, M, Rego and Rimbui, Z (1998)
    Environmental  Education: Essential knowledge for Sustainable
    Development. Longhorn
Odum, E.P. (1971)
Fundamentals of Ecology.  W.A Sanders.
Otiende, J.E. et al. (1991)
    Environmental Education Nairobi University Press
UNESCO (1980)
    Environmental Education in the Light of Tbilisi Conference

# 5

## CHAPTER 5

## KENYA'S ENVIRONMENTAL CRISIS

Introduction

In the previous chapter, you were introduced to the impact of development on the Earth's natural balance. You learned that while the Earth's resources provide the base for the satisfaction of human needs and want, the process of transformation leads to all manner of environmental degradation. In this chapter, you will examine the environmental problems afflicting Kenya and on the basis of these, you will examine the reasons for this and the possible strategies of enhancing the conservation and management of her environment. It is on this basis that we can say Kenya's environment is ecologically, socially, economically and politically stressed.

**Expected Learning Outcomes**

By the end of the topic learners should be able to:

- Outline and discuss the various indicators of Kenya's ecologically

## Kenya's Ecologically Stressed Environment

Kenya covers an area of about 587,000 km² of which 11,000 km² is covered by water. However, her environment is stressed and in a state of crisis in terms of ecological, political, social and economic dimensions. Some of the indices of the state of Kenya's environment are outlined in this section. We also examine the interventions being put in place to improve the quality of the environment.

## Change in Quality and Quantity of Water Resources

The major water catchments areas in Kenya (also known as water towers) include Mau Hills, Aberdare Mountains, Chereng'any Hills, Mt. Elgon, Mt. Kenya, Chyulu Hills, Taita Hills (Eastern Arc mountains). These are sources of important permanent rivers in the country. For example, the following rivers flow from Chereng'any Hills i.e. Sosiani, Chepkoilel and Tarach. There are many rivers and streams that emanate from Mt. Elgon that drain into River Nzoia that empties into Lake Victoria. The Aberdare Mountains are the main source of several streams that sustain Lakes Bogoria and Baringo, while the Chyulu Hills are the source of the Mzima springs that supply the whole of Mombasa, Kwale and Kilifi counties with water.

Deforestation for timber, fuelwood, charcoal burning, and to allow space for farming and settlement, that has occurred in the water catchment areas of Mt. Kenya, the Aberdares, Mau Hills, Mt. Elgon and Kaptagat forests have negatively impacted on these watersheds. The water flow in the rivers and streams and the volume in the lakes have been decreasing. There is now reduced water availability, the inability of the water catchment areas to regulate run-off leading to flooding, severe erosion, siltation of water systems, less volume of water in rivers and diminished re-charge of underground water resources. Consequently, the functions of ecological catchments have been greatly impaired.

It is therefore not surprising that the rivers and streams are drying up including rivers Athi, Tana, Yala, Nyando, Miriu, Kerio, Turwell and Nzoia. Similarly, all the lakes are reducing in terms of water levels. They include lakes Nakuru, Elementaita, Baringo, Naivasha, Turkana and Bogoria. This reduction in the quantity of water in these major wetlands is attributed to the increase in deforestation and settlements in water catchment areas. For example, lakes Nakuru, Elementaita, and Naivasha and several rivers associated with them are reducing in size mainly due to the deforestation of the Mau and Aberdare forests which form one of the

Karuru Falls in the Aberdare Mountains, Kenya. Photo/ORIENTALIZING/FLICKR

country's major water catchment areas.

Water levels in some lakes and rivers are also falling due to indiscriminate use of water for irrigation, and for livestock, domestic and industrial uses without proper planning, monitoring and management. This could partly explain the reducing water levels in lakes Naivasha and River Tana. For example, Lake Naivasha is surrounded by many large flower farms like Oserian, Homegrown, Sher Agencies and the Delamere farm which abstract a lot of water for irrigation. The same farms use a variety of fertilisers and pesticides that are causing pollution on the same lake hence affecting the quality of water which has, in turn, experienced reduced fish stocks affecting the fisher folk who depended on it for their livelihoods.

The Lake Victoria water hyacinth crisis can be viewed as both local and regional as the water resource is shared by Kenya, Uganda and Tanzania. The proliferation of the weed on the Kenyan side has been blamed on the increase in levels of phosphorus and nitrogen coming from fertilisers being used in the tea farms in Kericho and other surrounding farms. The weed has impeded fishing activities while the fish stocks have also dwindled due to the reduction of biological oxygen.

## Intervention Measures

To reduce the emerging crises of catchment degradation, the government has put in place policy, legal and institutional mechanisms to mitigate the impacts. These include the Environmental Management and Coordination Act (EMCA), 1999, the Water Act (2002), establishment and operationalisation of the National Environment Management Authority

84

(NEMA) and the Water Resources Management Authority (WRMA). The 'basin development authorities' were created to manage some of these lakes and rivers. However, these have not been very effective due to mismanagement, corruption and lack of foresight. These include Lake Victoria Basin Development Authority (LBDA), Kerio Valley Development Authority (KVDA), Tana and Athi River Development Authority (TARDA), and Ewasonyiro River Development Authority.

## Increased Deforestation

Over the years, the forest cover in Kenya has declined from 18% at independence in 1963 to about 1.8% at the moment. This is attributed to clearing of trees for settlement and agriculture, timber and construction materials, extraction of forest products, and fuelwood, especially charcoal production. With restricted access to gazetted forests, deforestation has mainly been experienced in arable and marginal (ASAL) lands. The demand for charcoal and timber has contributed immensely to the loss of trees. The consequences of deforestation have already been discussed elsewhere in this book. However, one consequence that must be mentioned here is the destabilisation of the water cycle. Increased deforestation interferes with the water cycle as less water is drawn from the ground, hence fewer clouds are formed. This is facilitated by the presence of increased dust particles in the atmosphere. Largely due to this, rains are becoming rarer while droughts are becoming more frequent and more prolonged. Whenever the rains come they tend to be torrential in nature.

## Desertification

Arid and Semi-arid lands (ASAL) of Kenya cover about 48.0 million hectares or about 75% of the country's total land surface area. About 9.6 ha are part of the marginal lands and can support agriculture. Increased desertification is observed particularly in the semi-arid or marginal lands. The counties within which marginal lands are found include Kitui, Makueni, Machakos, Narok, Kajiado, Isiolo, Marsabit, Nanyuki, Kwale, Samburu, Laikipia, Garissa and Taita Taveta.

In the fragile dryland ecosystems, land degradation is due to devegetation through over-grazing, uncontrolled burning, fuelwood and charcoal burning, intensive cultivation, installation of water points, and settlement. These activities lead to the destruction of indigenous vegetation and even the remaining stock of these trees are dying due to the reversing desert conditions. The setting in of desert-like conditions or **desertification** greatly reduces land capability to support human, animal, and plant life. In Narok County, for example, huge tracts of land have been

Wheat farming in Narok County, Kenya. Signs of desertification are being experienced in Narok County because huge tracts of land are under cultivation. Photo/NJOROGE THUO/FLICKR

put under wheat or maize or livestock cultivation and the whole area is slowly becoming a desert. Indigenous vegetation has been destroyed for this purpose and desert conditions are setting in. Desertification leads to problems that threaten the natural resource base and the sustainability of ecosystems that support life. This is expressed in soil erosion and water pollution due to siltation, and reduced agriculture productivity, carrying capacity of grazing lands, water quantity and quality, and fuelwood output. Kenya's survival depends on how best we use our ASAL areas, which account for about 75% of our land surface. The ASAL project which was initiated by the government to manage these lands has not been effective but needs to be reactivated.

## Shrinking Wetlands

Wetlands are defined by the Ramsar Convention as "areas of marsh, fern, wetland or water, whether natural or artificial, permanent or temporary with water that is static or flowing, fresh, brackish or salt, including areas of marine water the depth of which at low tides does not exceed six metres." Going by this definition, wetlands in Kenya cover marine and coastal wetlands and inland freshwater, including lakes, rivers and swamps, alkaline and saline lakes and constructed wetlands like dams. They occupy about 3% to 4% of the land surface and up to 6% during the rainy season.

Some of the wetlands include western Kenya inland water ecosystems such as Lake Victoria basin, Yala swamps, Sio Port swamps, rivers Nzoia, Miriu, Nyando and associated swamps, support a large variety

The rehabilitation of Nairobi river in 2007. Photo/YUSUNKWON/FLICKR

of fauna and flora with varied physical and chemical features; Rift Valley wetlands include Lake Nakuru, Ewaso Nyiro South, Saiwa swamp, Lake Kamnarok, Lake Naivasha, Lake Baringo, Lake Bogoria, Lake Elementaita, Lake Magadi, Lake Turkana, Lotikipi plains, Lake Amboseli, Lake Oloiden, Lake Sonachi and Lake Solai. Others around Nairobi include Lake Simek (seasonal lake); Kimana, Namelok, Ongarua site, Manguo, Ruiru, Ewaso swamp/Shompolen (permanent swamps); Nagolomon, Nairobi, Njumbi, Hyena, Ruai, Karen, Athi basin, Kingfisher, Olomanyi, Eland, Hippo pools, Ondiri (constructed dams). Others are spread over different parts of the country.

Wetlands act as water storage, flood control, water filtration, recharge and discharge and pollution control systems. They are highly productive and rich in unique biodiversity. Some communities use wetlands for the supply of herbal medicine and to conduct traditional rites. They are key resources for sustainable development especially poverty reduction and improvement of livelihood for communities in terms of provision of water for agriculture, livestock, and domestic use and raw materials for crafts.

Many of the wetlands are progressively being degraded. Some swamps and marshes have been drained to allow for agriculture and settlement. Many Rivers and streams are experiencing reduced water levels due to deforestation of the water catchment areas. Many dams originally developed for use by communities during the colonial era have been neglected and some have dried up, many others continue to suffer from siltation. The degradation of wetlands reduces their capacity to act as water storage, to control floods, to filter water or to act as sinks to pollution. The rich and unique biodiversity has been disrupted and many species of plants and animals have become extinct or are threatened with extinction. Communities who previously relied on them for the supply of herbal medicine and to conduct traditional rites are completely disadvantaged at the loss of biodiversity.

## Destruction of Biodiversity

Kenya is rich in biodiversity which occupies a wide array of ecosystems including marine, coastal, freshwater and inland saline lakes. Coastal and marine biodiversity include mangroves, seagrasses, seaweeds, coral reefs, marine fishes, molluscs, reptiles, crustaceans, coastal birds, turtles, and marine mammals. Forests, covering 6,687,390 hectares, support a huge collection of biodiversity. Inland water ecosystems such as Lake Victoria basin, Yala swamps, Sio Port swamps, Lake Amboseli and associated swamps, also support a large variety of fauna and flora with varied physical and chemical features.

The Kenya Wildlife Service (KWS) is mandated to conserve and manage wildlife since this resource has both monetary and aesthetic values. National parks, marine national parks, nature reserves, national reserves, game sanctuaries, forest reserves, Ramsar sites and proposed protected areas all occupy an area of 6,103,288 hectares. Wildlife in Kenya is reducing in large numbers and many are now endangered species including Hippos, African elephants (20 years ago, they were 145,000; today there are only 20,000), rhinos (20 years ago, they were 20,000; today they are less than 600), ostriches, flamingoes, lions, leopards and cheetahs. Many of these are killed through illegal hunting and poisoning by solid wastes deposited in some national parks. For example, in the Nairobi National Park, pollution from Athi River cement factory and chemical wastes have forced animals out of their habitats and several others have died due to the pollution. Others are killed through habitat fragmentation and degradation and transmission of diseases from livestock and vice versa.

Indigenous plants particularly traditional medicinal and food plants such as vegetables and mushrooms are disappearing. The Neem tree is endangered as well as a number of Acacia family trees that are being harvested by wood carvers at the Coast of Kenya. *Brachyleana hulliensis* has been classified as endangered. This is mainly due to uninformed destruction of the plants. This leads to the destruction of important genetic resources which would prove to be beneficial to humankind in the future.

The loss of biodiversity in the Kenyan environment leads to several problems. First, biodiversity is essential for the sustainable functioning of agricultural, forest, and natural ecosystems upon which human survival and health depend. The loss of a key species (e.g., loss of a predator) creates an imbalance among the remaining species, and can sometimes result in the collapse of the entire ecosystem. Altering a habitat may also improve the environment for infectious diseases, like dengue. Second, species diversity also affects the quantity and quality of human food supply. For example, conserving pollinators and natural enemies of pests is essential for successful grain, fruit, and vegetable production. Loss of biodiversity leads to reduced access to food sources and increased instances of malnutrition. Thirdly, gene pools are being destroyed as well as medicinal plants. Many plants and animals carry potentially useful genetic information an example being the discovery of Penicillin which came from a fungus.

## Destruction of the Lithosphere

Soil is a significant non-renewable natural resource that supports life through such activities as agriculture. Land degradation is the reduction of the land capability to satisfy a particular use. This could be attributed to inappropriate land use, overgrazing, deforestation, poor irrigation, over-exploitation of aquifers, intensive tillage and cropping, recurrent droughts, climate change and mining.

Land degradation manifests in loss or degradation of soil, fauna, flora, water and biological productivity in areas under ecological stress. Soil erosion in Kenya is rampant due to the destruction of vegetation leaving the soil vulnerable to erosion whenever it rains. Soil erosion renders the soil infertile.

The soil is also being destroyed through unplanned mining of the soil, such as brick making in western Kenya (Vihiga and Kakamega counties). This has led to the loss of topsoil and loam soil and has an added consequence of destroying trees as they are used for firing the bricks.

Soil erosion leads to frequent floods whenever it rains due to increased siltation of rivers and streams arising from rapid soil deposition in the rivers. Floods cause a lot of destruction to property and biodiversity and also the loss of human life.

## Increased Pollution

Increase of soil, water and air pollution is being experienced throughout the Kenya environment. Activities related to energy production, distribution, and consumption are the largest single sources of air pollution. Indoor air pollution is largely due to the emission of smoke and particulates from the burning of biomass fuel such as wood, crop residues, and dung, for cooking or, heating water. The smoke contains pollutants, especially benzo-a-pyrene and formaldehyde. The consumption of fossil fuel by industry and automobiles, which averages 2.3 million tonnes per year and when burnt releases vast quantities of emissions into the atmosphere, is the most contributing factor to air pollution. Outdoor air pollution is mainly due to some of the emissions in the smoke particles from factories and automobiles containing sulphur and particulates. Increased air pollution is also partly due to increased dust particles in the atmosphere due to increased bare grounds as a result of vegetation destruction and mining activities. The most notable mining activities include sand harvesting, quarrying for dimension stones, aggregates, ballast and other soft minerals like limestone, dolomite, and kaolin. The mining of minerals contributes to the problem as well, including diatomite at Gilgil, titanium in Kwale, cement at Bamburi, and Athi river, trona and common salt at Lake Magadi, and fluorspar in Kerio Valley. Air pollution, in general, has been linked to acute respiratory tract infections. For example, dust particles lead to various problems such as respiratory diseases and other airborne diseases as well as different kinds of cancers.

Water and land pollution are mainly due to increased deposits of chemical and solid wastes from industries. Webuye paper factory, Bamburi and Athi river cement, Thika factories, Nairobi industrial area factories, Dagoretti and Kawangware abattoirs, are some of the major culprits of water and land pollution. Others include agro-based industries such as flower production, sugar industries, coffee industries, and tanning industries. These industries use a variety of chemical pollutants which are released as effluents into the water and soil. For example, methyl bromide, an ozone layer depleting chemical, is used as a fumigant in the flower farms.

## Energy Crisis

The energy types used in Kenya include wood fuel (75%), fossil fuels (18%), hydro and geothermal power (1.4%) and others such as wind, radioactive minerals, and solar energy (0.2%). About 67% of all households use firewood while 46% use charcoal. The over-reliance on biomass fuels can be attributed to the high levels of poverty; a greater proportion of Kenyans cannot afford alternative fuels and have to depend on natural biomass for their energy needs. Over 80% of the wood used is from the renewable stock of agro-forestry and other on-farm systems such as homestead trees, community trees and wood plantations, with only 16% derived from trust lands and gazetted forests. Industries such as cottage, coffee, tea, tobacco, dairy and sugar also use firewood. It has become necessary to increase access to electricity, particularly in rural areas to lessen the strain on biomass fuel sources. In addition, many more factories and the transport sector have experienced increased use of fossil fuels causing a frequent shortage of petrol and petroleum products.

With the increase in population, demand for energy supply has been growing by 5% annually. This has placed heavy pressure on the existing sources of energy. The diminishing supply of energy in Kenya, both wood fuel and electricity, due to increased demand, affects the whole country, hence referred to as a national crisis. The problem is manifested in increased deforestation and frequent power failures in the country. The energy crisis due to the diminishing supply of fossil energy since the 1970s constitutes a global environmental crisis and merits attention by the whole world community.

## Social Degradation

Society is undergoing drastic changes as expressed by increased poverty, crime, cases of mental disorders, cases of drug addiction, lack of patriotism, corruption, indiscipline among the youth, cultural miscegenation (confused cultures), and cases of violence both domestic and the mob. Several factors contribute to this situation.

First, is the rampant poverty in the country due to the lack of proper policies in the distribution of wealth. Over 57 % of Kenyans live in abject poverty with incomes of less than USD3 per month. They do not have access to quality food, shelter, clothing, education, healthcare, water, sanitation, and entertainment. They are therefore forced to engage in activities that degrade the environment, such as mindless destruction of vegetation for farming and poor farming methods that lead to soil erosion and promotion of poor sanitation. They, therefore, experience psychological stress that motivates them to commit crime, resign to drug and alcohol abuse and even to suffer mental disorders.

Second, are the influence of the media both print (magazines, newspapers, brochures, etc) and electronic (TV, films, videos, Facebook, Twitter, internet). The messages and images in these media channels influence the thinking and actions of Kenyans, especially the youth, to abandon many socially recognised values and beliefs for Western values and practices. The result is cultural miscegenation that often throws the youth in conflict with the mainstream society.

Third, is the lack of adequate meaningful counselling policies in our lives and lack of meaningful cultural education. There is an urgent need to make counselling services available to Kenyans on a wide range of issues such as wealth creation, management of resources, stress management, time management, conflict resolution and management, among others. Cultural education at formal and informal levels would also be necessary to help Kenyans appreciate their cultures and values and to develop personal social skills.

## Summary

In this chapter, you have learned about the human factor in the Earth's environmental crisis. You learned that environmental crisis implies that the environment is deeply affected but it can be salvaged if corrective measures are taken in good time. You also learned that the environmental problems we experience today in Kenya are a result of many years of human interaction with the environment. The magnitude of the problems depends on the level of social organisation and the technological advancement of society. Kenya's environment is ecologically, economically, and socially stressed thus undermining the foundation of its political base.

## End of Chapter Activities

Outline the environmental problems afflicting Kenya and make suggestions for improvement.

## Bibliography

National Environment Authority (2004)
       State of Environment Report 2003, Kenya. Nairobi: National
       Environment Authority

# 6

## CHAPTER 6

## POLICIES AND STRATEGIES FOR SUSTAINABLE DEVELOPMENT

### Introduction

In the previous chapters, you were introduced to the major reasons for the environmental crises we experience today throughout the world, Kenya included. The overriding factor has been the nature of the development model that focuses majorly on ecological exploitation for the purpose of economic gains but ignoring the social and political dimensions of the environment. In this chapter, you will learn about the need for sustainable development and the various ways in which societies may adopt sustainable living for the purpose of preserving the stability of ecosystems, social coherence, and economic and political sustainability.

### Meaning of Sustainable Development

Sustainable development is the development that meets the need and aspirations of the present generation without compromising the ability of future generations to meet their own needs.

Sustainable development, a term popularised by **Our Common Future**, the 1987 report of the World Commission on Environment and Development, chaired by Gro Harlem Brundtland, means '*meeting the needs of the present without compromising the ability of future generations to meet their own needs*'. The definition has been widely criticised as being ambiguous and prone to different interpretations. An important document called ***Caring for the Earth*** (1981) makes an even better this definition by stating that sustainable development means: '*improving the quality of human life while living within the carrying capacity of supporting ecosystems*'. Thus a **sustainable economy** is the product of sustainable development. It maintains its natural resource base and can continue to develop by adapting, and through improvements in knowledge, organisation, and technical efficiency.

Sustainable development then means progress in human well-being that can be prolonged over many generations than just a few years. Its benefits must be available to all humans rather than to just the members of a privileged group. It thus promises to alleviate acute poverty while also guaranteeing environmental quality.

## Sustainability: New Applications

The concept of sustainable development is derived from the term "sustainable". If an activity is sustainable, then it can continue forever. The term sustainability ensues from the word sustainable.

However, there can be no long-term guarantee of sustainability of any activity because many factors involved in the activity may be unknown and largely unpredictable. The term sustainability is today applied to many situations e.g. sustainable living, sustainable growth, sustainable use, sustainable economy, sustainable society, sustainable human progress, sustainable schools, sustainable universities, sustainable marriage among others.

"**Sustainable use**" applies only to renewable resources in which they are used at rates within their capacity for renewal, while "**sustainable economy**" refers to a product of sustainable development in which the natural resource base is maintained and it can continue to develop by adapting, and through improvements in knowledge, organisation, technological efficiency, and wisdom.

**Sustainable society** refers to the society that practices the principles for sustainable living in their day to day lives.

**Sustainability** is the quest for a sustainable society, one that can persist over generations without destroying the social and life-supporting systems that current and future generations of humans (and all other species on Earth) depend on (Australian Government, 2005). Sustainability entails a process of people reflecting on their present relationships with each other and with the natural environment and its implication for future generations (Ndaruga, 2014). Creation of a sustainable future is an essential response to the current state of the world's ecosystems. To achieve **sustainability,** some things – jobs, productivity, wages, capital, savings, profits, information, knowledge, education, social welfare and justice – must grow, while others – pollution, waste and poverty – must decline.

**Sustainability**, according to UNESCO (2006), relates to ways of thinking about the world and forms of social and personal practice that lead to:

- Ethical, empowered and personally fulfilled individuals;
- Communities built on collaborative engagement, tolerance and equity;
- Social systems and institutions that are participatory, and just; and
- Environmental practices that value and sustain biodiversity and life-supporting ecological processes.

Based on these dimensions, we all need to embrace sustainability by:

- Being conservative in actions that could affect the environment; and
- Studying the effects of such actions carefully and learn from our mistakes.

Sustainability when applied institutionally within a school, is the development of a process or management system that helps to create a vibrant school economy and a high quality of life while respecting the need to sustain natural resources and protect the environment, Sustainability programmes are those that result from an institution's commitment to environmental, social and economic health or the "triple bottom line". Thus sustainability has both individual and institutional applicability and is usually a balancing act.

**Sustainability** acknowledges the ecological, economic, social and political dimensions that can inhibit or support the capacity of individuals, communities or nations to properly care for the environment. It also seeks to promote stewardship of the environment, encouraging everyone to assume responsibility of caring for the environment. In principle, sustainability focuses on community, inclusiveness, moderation in living, basics in life, and connectedness.

## The Relevance of Sustainability to Project Management

Sustainability is certainly relevant to project planning and management in the following subtle ways including studying both the living and non-living environment, understanding ecosystems and effective operations so that projects do not destabilise the balance, and so that the use of resources is balanced over time.

## Need for Sustainable Development

Economic growth is the best way to bring about a long-range transformation to more advanced and productive societies and to provide resources to improve the livelihood of all people. Using ever-increasing amounts of goods and services to make human life more comfortable, pleasant, or agreeable must inevitably interfere with the survival of other species, and eventually, of humans themselves in a world of finite resources. Economic growth is therefore impossible in the long run because of the limits imposed by non-renewable resources (which are finite) and the capacity of the biosphere to absorb our wastes which result in an unhealthy environment.

This means that security and living standards for the world's population are inextricably linked to environmental protection. While development leads to improved lives of the people, our greatest challenge is to continue improving human welfare within the limits of the Earth's natural resources; we have to promote **sustainable development.**

Creation of a sustainable future is an essential response to the current state of the world's ecosystems. To achieve sustainability, some things – jobs, productivity, wages, capital, savings, profits, information, knowledge, education, social welfare and justice – must grow, while others – pollution, waste and poverty – must decline.

Sustainability acknowledges the ecological, economic, social and political dimensions that can inhibit or support the capacity of individuals, communities or nations to properly care for the environment. It also seeks to promote stewardship of the environment, encouraging everyone to assume responsibility of caring for the environment.

Economic growth is the best way to bring about a long-range transformation to more advanced and productive societies and to provide resources to improve the lives of all people. Using ever-increasing amounts of goods and services to make human life more comfortable, pleasant, or agreeable must inevitably interfere with the survival of other species, and eventually, of humans themselves in a world of finite resources. Economic growth is therefore impossible in the long run because of the limits imposed by non-renewable resources (which are finite) and the capacity of the biosphere to absorb our wastes which result in an unhealthy environment.

This means that security and living standards for the world's population are inextricably linked to environmental protection. While development leads to improved lives of the people, our greatest challenge is to continue improving human welfare within the limits of the Earth's natural resources; we have to promote **sustainable development.**

---

### Box 6.1

#### Discussion

Do you now understand that sustainability has three interlinked spheres, namely environmental or ecological, social and economic?

The **social dimension** is in terms of the level of quality of life that is influenced by the economic practices of the people. The pattern of production that cares little about the extraction and use of resources to produce innumerable goods and services in planned or perceived obsolescence encourages heavy pollution of the environment (**environmental dimension**) as well as a high level of consumption (consumerism). Consumption becomes a way of life whereby goods and services are bought and used for rituals, burnt, replaced, and discarded in an accelerating manner. We listen more to the satisfaction of our ego rather than to our spiritual satisfaction (**social dimension)**. The consumption pattern leads to a waste disposal problem that further destroys the quality of the environment. Thus unsustainable communities are a result of economic, social and environmental factors. How do we arrive at sustainability? This question is answered through the **Education for Sustainable Development.**

---

## Concerns of Sustainable Development

The following are the objectives for sustainable development:

- Balanced growth, that takes into account improvement in the quality of life and that of the environment;
- Reviving economic growth. Sustainable growth is dependent on

each nation achieving its full economic potential, while at the same time enhancing the environmental resource base upon which development must be based;

- Changing the quality of economic growth to focus more on meeting the essential needs for jobs, energy, water, sanitation; ensuring a sustainable level of population; conserving and enhancing the resource base; re-orienting technology and managing risk; and merging environment and economics in decision making;
- Meeting the basic needs of humanity such as food, clothing, shelter and jobs. This involves paying attention to the largely unmet needs of the world's poor;
- Proper planning in the development programmes;
- Cost-effective development;
- Promotion of people-centred development programmes;
- Healthy and secure environment for all;
- Using resources sparingly; and
- Self-reliance and environmental stewardship by all.

Changing the quality of growth requires changes in traditional economic thinking in which the process of economic development is more based on the realities of the stock capital that sustains it. For example, income from forestry operations is conventionally measured in terms of the value of timber and other products extracted minus the costs of extraction. The costs of regenerating the forest are not taken into account when money is actually spent on such work. This is the case of the incomplete account occurs in the exploitation of other natural resources that if they are not capitalised in enterprise or national accounts such as water, air and soil.

Economic development must take full account in its measurement of growth of the improvements or deterioration of the stock of natural resources. This requires economic account through merging of environmental considerations into economic planning and decision making. Thus sustainable development is not a fixed state but a process of change in which the exploitation of resources, the direction of investments, the orientation of technological development, and institutional change are all in harmony and enhance both current and future of potential to meet human needs and aspirations.

## Principles of Sustainable Development

A 'sustainable society' lives by the principles of sustainable development. These principles are elaborated in the document, **Caring for the Earth** and also in the **Earth Charter**.

The following are the key principles of environmental management.

- Integrated Management: Attempting to provide a national framework for integration of ecological, economic, political and social dimensions in a unified systems approach in the development process. This is because we cannot have sustained progress towards social goals in a deteriorating environment or economy and vice versa;
- Respect Earth and life in all its diversity: Providing information, skills and attitudes that enable communities and individuals to participate in environmental management with full knowledge of its purpose, to elicit change in terms of sustainability and to spur them to action;
- Promotion of Global Alliance: Adopting means of production throughout the world that increase the benefits from available resources and maintain natural wealth. Such are the means that look for products that are affordably made by simple production methods from local materials for local use and that advocate safe, creative, environmentally sound, emotionally satisfying work conducted in conditions of human dignity and freedom that creates social bonds rather than breaking them apart. This means that we have partnered with, and network with the people, throughout the world, create sustainable livelihoods suitable for prevailing conditions in order to avoid future environmental damage and to strengthen the foundations of global environmental security;
- People Participation: Generating meaningful stakeholder and public involvement and facilitate collective decision making with a view to promoting democracy, nonviolence and peace among communities. This is because people cannot be separated from nature. They inescapably affect ecological patterns and processes and are in turn affected by them;
- Conservation of Ecological Integrity: Considering the protection of the whole environment in terms of all levels of biodiversity hierarchy (genes, species, populations, ecosystems and landscapes), maintenance of essential ecological processes and life support systems, i.e. conservation of the earth's vitality and diversity;
- Promotion of Social and Economic Justice: Considering human needs and promoting sustainable economic development and equitable development of communities with a view to eradicating poverty, gender disparity, and discrimination of all sorts and thus

improve the quality of people's lives. In this way, it is also possible to promote intra and inter-generational equity. To achieve sustainability, some things such as job creation, productivity, wages, profits, knowledge, social welfare and social justice – must, therefore, grow, while others – pollution, waste, poverty and inequitable distribution of wealth – must decline;

- Care for the Community of life: Providing information, skills and attitudes that enable communities and individuals to participate in environmental management with full knowledge of its purpose, to elicit change in terms of sustainability and to spur them to action; and
- Precautionary Approach: Minimising the depletion of non-renewable resources and keep within the earth's carrying capacity. The principle of polluter pays should be applied as a deterrent action against the unnecessary use of non-renewable resources. To achieve sustainability, some things – jobs, productivity, wages, capital, savings, profits, knowledge, education, social welfare and justice – must grow, while others – pollution, waste and poverty – must decline. Proper planning is therefore mandatory.

## Constraints on Sustainable Development in African Countries

It is believed that there is no realistic hope of developing nations reaching the present standard of living of developed nations due to certain limits to development such as low level of initial capital to develop industries, low levels of technology, lack of adequate nonrenewable resources, lack of adequate energy resources, social organisation, and the ability of the biosphere to absorb the effects of industrialisation. The constraints are thus technological, social, ecological, economic, and political.

**Technological constraints**: Many African countries do not have a critical mass of trained personnel nor the instrumental capacity for generation and adaptation of technologies in order to make them appropriate for executing sustainable development programmes. The limits of development are not absolute but are imposed by present states of technology and social organisation and by their impacts on environmental resources and upon the biosphere's ability to absorb the effects of human activities.

**Political constraints**: These include the colonial legacy and the dependence syndrome, political instability that wards of economic investments, corruption and inefficiency in governance, poor or lack of appropriate planning, inappropriate policies and strategies, deficiencies in legal and legislative support for development programmes, and lack of effective regional integration and collaboration in development.

**Social constraints:** Deficiencies in education and training, lack of specific training programmes in environmental management and resources inventory, lack of an effective campaign and advocacy with regard to public sensitisation and orientation about sustainable development, high levels of poverty, social organisation, and gender disparities in education.

**Economic constraints**: Unfavourable economic conditions due to heavy debt burden, negative effects of structural adjustment programmes and several decades of continued decline in commodity prices, and limited financial support for sustainable development programmes.

**Ecological Constraints**: Lack of adequate non-renewable resources, lack of adequate water and energy resources, and the inability of the biosphere to absorb the effects of industrialisation.

In summary, the constraints include:

- Corruption and deficiencies in governance;
- Political instability and lack of focused political leadership;
- Poor planning;
- Inappropriate policies and strategies;
- Gaps in legal and legislative support for development programmes;
- Lack of adequate regional integration and collaboration in development;
- Deficiencies in education and training;
- Poverty and adverse economic conditions;
- Lack of awareness about a new paradigm in development incorporating sustainable development; and
- Inappropriate technology and lack of technical support.

## Conditions for Sustainable Development

The pursuit of sustainable development requires the following conditions:

- A political system that secures effective citizen participation in decision making;
- An economic system that is able to generate surpluses and technological knowledge on a self-reliant and sustained basis;
- A social system that provided for solutions for the tensions arising from disharmonised development;
- Creation of a more equitable global economic order;

- A production system that respects the obligation to preserve the ecological base for development;
- A technological system that can search continuously for new solutions;
- An international system that fosters sustainable patterns of trade and finance;
- An administrative system that is flexible and has the capacity for self-correction;
- Stop using up the earth's ecological capital and begin to draw on the interest gotten from the sustainable husbandry of the resources;
- Governments making the concept of sustainable development central to all planning activities;
- All nations adopting new, more equitable, an international economic structure that begins to narrow the gap between the developed and developing nations; and
- Integrating economic and ecological considerations into development planning.

## Indicators of Sustainability

A sustainable society enables its members to achieve a high quality of life in ways that are ecologically sustainable. The indicators of quality of life and of ecological sustainability include the following:

### Quality of Life

This includes the Human Development Index (HDI) and Human Development Freedom (HDF). HDI has three components:

- Longevity (life expectancy);
- Knowledge level in terms of adult literacy; and
- Income in terms of per capita Gross Domestic Product.

### Ecological Sustainability

A society is ecologically sustainable when it:

- Conserves ecological life-support systems and biodiversity;
- Ensures that uses of renewable resources are sustainable and minimises the depletion of non-renewable resources; and
- Keeps within the carrying capacity of supporting ecosystems.

a) Implementation of environmental education for sustainability in Kenya

- Development of ESD implementation strategy (2005-2014) by NEMA; in collaboration with other stakeholders;
- Encouraging every sector of the economy to mainstream ESD in their activities; through the development of specific sector ESD strategies;
- NEMA has developed environmental education resource materials; to sensitise various stakeholders on ESD - e.g. booklets, brochures, posters, stickers, magazines with a specific message relevant to events and occasions;
- Establishing modalities by NEMA for public participation in environmental management activities; with sustainability in mind; these include:

  - Collaboration with civil society organisation;
  - Collaboration with media on diverse topics resulting in the publication of articles, supplements, talk shows documentaries in both print and electronic media;
  - Partnership with the private sector, in activities such as clean-ups, support to events such as WED, etc; and
  - Gazettement of environmental inspectors, who help in ensuring compliance with the environmental standard.

b) How the government of Kenya is encouraging sustainable development

- Environmental conservation programmes e.g afforestation;
- Encouraging green energy production and use;
- Carbon trading programmes;
- Proper environmental planning supported by legislation;
- Public participation in economic and environmental programs;
- Environmental impact assessment of development projects;
- Intra and inter-generational equality programmes;
- Gender mainstreaming and affirmative action;
- Economic stimulus programmes;
- Encouraging recycling and re-using of resources; and

- Environmental education for sustainability as spearheaded by NEMA

## Summary

In this chapter, you learned about the need for sustainable development and the various ways in which societies may adopt sustainable living for the purpose of preserving the stability of ecosystems, social coherence, and economic and political sustainability. It is now clear that the term sustainable development has been expanded in the application and its now common to refer to sustainability. Many countries have put in place mechanisms to adopt sustainability in their day to day operations.

## End of Chapter Activities

- Differentiate between sustainable development and sustainability;
- Provide reasons why sustainable development should be adopted in the development process of any community;
- What programme would you put in place to take care of the needs of the special needs children in line with the requirements for social sustainability?;
- Outline the ways in which sustainable development can be achieved; and
- Provide some of the constraints against the achievement of sustainable development.

## Bibliography

Department of Environment, Government of NCT of Delhi and CLEAN-INDIA (no date) **The Earth Charter for Delhi Schools.** New Delhi: Bhagidari

IUCN/ UNEP/ WWF (1991)
**Caring for the Earth. A Strategy for Sustainable Living**. Gland, Switzerland: IUCN/ UNEP/ WWF

Ndaruga, Ayub Macharia(2014).
Education for Sustainable Development(ESD) Explained. Nairobi: TechLearn Institute

**The Earth Charter,**
http://www.earthcharter.org/files/charter/charter**, pdf**
The World Commission on Environment and Development (1987) Our Common Future. Oxford: Oxford University Press

UNESCO (2006)

    Framework for the United Nations Decade of Education for Sustainable Development: International Implementation Scheme. Paris: UNESCO.

# 7

## CHAPTER 7

## EDUCATION FOR SUSTAINABLE DEVELOPMENT (ESD)

### Introduction

This chapter focuses on Education for Sustainable Development (ESD). This is the type of education that seeks to integrate the key values inherent in sustainable development, espoused in the various documents such as the Earth Charter and Caring for the Earth, into all aspects of learning to encourage changes in behaviour that allow more sustainable living. ESD is a precursor to environmental education for sustainability; every effort should be made to understand its basic structure and philosophy as a basis for environmental education for sustainability.

**Expected Learning Outcomes**

By the end of this topic you should be able to:

- Demonstrate an understanding of the significance of ESD as a driver of sustainability;
- Outline the dimensions of the concept of sustainability;
- Relate the content of ESD to the dynamics of education and sustainability; and
- Demonstrate an understanding of the key features of ESD.

## Meaning of Education for Sustainable Development (ESD)

ESD originated from the recommendation reached at the World Summit on Sustainable Development held in Johannesburg in 2002 that recognised education as being critical for sustainable development and as a key agent for change. The plan of implementation of the Summit recommended that the UN General Assembly consider adopting a Decade of Education for Sustainable Development starting in 2005 (www.unesco.org/education/desd). Following the summit, the UN General Assembly adopted resolution 57/254 to put in place a UN Decade of Education for Sustainable Development (DESD), lasting from 2005 to 2014. UNESCO was tasked with leading the Decade and developing a draft International Implementation Scheme for the Decade. *The overall goal of DESD is to integrate the values inherent in sustainable development into all aspects of learning to encourage changes in behaviour that allow for a more sustainable and just society (UNESCO, 2006).*

ESD is essentially the integration of the key values inherent in sustainable development, espoused in the various documents such as the Earth Charter and Caring for the Earth, into all aspects of learning to encourage changes in behaviour that allow more sustainable living.

The basic vision of DESD is a world where everyone has the opportunity to benefit from education and learn the values, behaviour and lifestyles required for a sustainable future and for positive societal transformation.

The objectives of DESD are to:

- Give an enhanced profile to the central role of education and learning in the common pursuit of sustainable development;
- Facilitate links and networking, exchange and interaction among stakeholders in ESD;
- Provide space and opportunity for refining and promoting the vision of, and transition to sustainable development through all forms of learning and public awareness;

- Foster increased quality of teaching and learning in education for sustainable development;
- Develop strategies at every level to strengthen capacity in ESD.

ESD is fundamentally about values, with respect for others, diversity, environment, and resources of the planet Earth. It aims at moving us to adopt behaviours and practices that enable all to live a full life without being deprived of basics.

Sustainable development consists of three key areas: Society; environment and economy.

- **Society** comprises of an understanding of social institutions and their role in change and development, as well as the democratic and participatory systems which give an opportunity for the expression of opinion, the selection of governments, the forging of consensus and the resolution of differences;
- **Environment** in terms of an awareness of the resources and fragility of the physical environment and the effects on it of human activity and decisions, with a commitment to factoring environmental concerns into social and economic policy development; and
- **Economy** consists of sensitivity to the limits and potential of economic growth and their impact on society, and on the environment, with a commitment to assess personal and societal levels of consumption out of concern for the environment and for social justice.

The **Bonn Declaration** at the UNESCO World Conference on Education for Sustainable Development held on 31st March to 2nd April 2009 reaffirmed the need for a shared commitment to education that empowers people for change in terms of achieving lifestyles based on economic and social justice, food security, ecological integrity, sustainable livelihoods, respect for all life forms and strong values that foster social cohesion, democracy and collective action. ESD was seen as a vehicle for this purpose since it is based on values, principles and practices necessary to respond effectively to current and future challenges. The Declaration outlined the key strategies for the implementation of ESD in all countries of the world including the formation of partnerships for capacity building across the world.

Education for sustainable development should not be equated with environmental education. The latter is a well-established discipline, which focuses on humankind's relationship with the natural environment and on ways to conserve and preserve it and properly steward its resources. According to Ndaruga (2014), a contest of economic, social, and cultural interests that people have, for example, on wetlands is also driven by consideration of the future generations. Consideration of the future makes education for sustainability different from conventional environmental education since this approach is more visionary, free from selfishness, collaborative and more respectful to other people and the natural environment. The practice of addressing the future issues through ESD leads to an examination of relationships, probable alternatives, appropriate empowerment and action as well as personal, professional, and political aspects that allow for a challenge of daily lifestyles, ambitions, and visions. The approach naturally gives students and members of the community to contemplate greener economic, social, and political dimensions of society (Tilbury, 1995:207). Education for Sustainable Development, therefore, encompasses environmental education, setting it in the broader context of socio-cultural factors and the socio-political issues of equity, poverty, democracy and quality of life.

---

**Box 7.1**

---

### Discussion

Do you note that Education for Sustainable Development (ESD) focuses on the integration of values inherent in sustainable development specifically applied to all aspects of learning to encourage changes in behaviour that allow more sustainable living? Education for sustainability includes many of the founding principles of environmental education but with a stronger human focus, recognizing that fundamental human rights and social justice are just as essential to sustainable development as environmental sustainability. Try to explain in your own words what the two components entail.

---

# Characteristic Features of Education for Sustainable Development

The following key features characterise Education for Sustainable Development (ESD):

- It is interdisciplinary and holistic (integrated) in nature - i.e. learning for sustainable development is embedded in the whole curriculum, not as a separate subject;
- It is values-driven;
- It's inclusive - no child or adult is left out;
- It is value – driven i.e. the values and principles underpinning sustainable development are identified, debated, and applied;
- It promotes critical thinking and problem solving that lead to confidence in addressing the dilemmas and challenges of sustainable development;
- Its goals and objectives are achieved through the use of different pedagogies that promote interaction between teachers and learners (interactive pedagogies) in an effort to improve the quality of the environment and the learning institutions together with the surrounding communities;
- It promotes participatory decision-making in what and how they learn;
- It encourages the application of ideas and knowledge in the day to day personal and professional life;
- It is problem-based/project-based/inquiry-based/evidence-based/experiential;
- It is conducted in a positive learning environment;
- Learners are allowed to learn from mistakes;
- It addresses local as well as global issues. The concepts of sustainable development are carefully selected and expressed in all the learning activities; and
- It should provide a scientific understanding of sustainability together with an understanding of values, principles, and lifestyles that will lead to the transition to sustainable development. This is best done by focusing more on the learning of science and technology, with the later applied with the goals of sustainability. Education that provides access to science and technology is an area where common cause should be made by advocating strongly for local input into how science and technology should be used.

Box 7.2

## Understanding Social Sustainability

Do you know that Special Education is the best example of upholding social sustainability? ESD takes into account the need to integrate children with special needs into mainstream society. The physically and mentally challenged children must be helped from the beginning to be integrated into society. This requires that the children are identified early enough to be introduced to special programmes that allow them to develop cognitive, affective and psychomotor abilities for the purpose.

The fundamental areas of concern include the provision of:

- Alternative communication using symbols, sign language, and writing;
- Treatment, particularly physiotherapy, occupational therapy and speech therapy;
- Wide-ranging skills including carpentry, salon, beauty care, swimming, and environmental protection such as harvesting of rainwater from roofs and distributing it for use in toilets, etc.

The teaching and learning activities take into account personal progression and small numbers in the classes (6-12 pupils) and the care of well-trained teachers and other personnel.

## The Core Content of ESD

Sustainable development is a complex undertaking, with connections to every part of life. The connections are broadly divided into socio-cultural, environmental or ecological, and economic perspectives. In planning and implementing ESD, it is important to maintain these connections so that the learning process gives people the chance to apply sustainable development principles across their lives and to understand the multiple impacts of their actions and behaviour.

The major themes that form the backbone of ESD content include:

- Sustainable consumption;
- Sustainable lifestyle;
- Cultural diversity;
- Health and quality of life;
- Water and energy;
- Biosphere reserves as places of learning;
- World heritage sites as places of learning;
- ESD in the knowledge society;
- Citizen participation and good governance;
- Poverty reduction and sustainable development projects; and
- Intergenerational justice and ethics.

The following 15 strategic pillars and the connections between them must inform education and learning for sustainable development (Table 7.1). Many of the perspectives are identified and explained in Agenda 21 and/or the Johannesburg plan of implementation as important concerns and challenges that need to be addressed in an effort to achieve sustainability.

**Table 7.1: The Core Content for ESD Programme**

| Broad Perspective | Strategic Pillars | Key Contents |
|---|---|---|
| Socio-cultural | Human Rights | Respect for human rights is a fundamental pillar for sustainable development; Need for the adoption of a rights-based approach to development; Need to assert the right to live in a sustainable environment; Lobbying and advocacy approach. |
| | Peace and human security | Peace and security are fundamental to human dignity and development; sustainable development is |

| | | undermined by insecurities and conflicts; these result in human tragedies, destruction of life and property, collapse of communities, health and education systems, communities, and social fabric; lead to displaced people and refugees; Provision of skills and values for peace in the minds of humanity. |
|---|---|---|
| | Gender Equality | Gender equality central to sustainable development where each member of society respects others and plays a role in which they can fulfil their potential and contribute to development; gender parity in education is central to the removal of social structures that perpetuate gender imbalance; Marginalisation due to gender reduces the chances of sustainable development; Need for mainstreaming of gender issues in education using suitable pedagogies for behavioural change. |
| | Cultural diversity and intercultural understanding | Understanding local cultures through proper learning strategies enable all communities to live in peace and harmony and play their role in the development process. |
| | Health | Ill-health hampers economic and social development leading to unsustainable resource use and environmental degradation. A healthy population and safe |

| | | environments are pre-conditions for sustainable development. Hunger, malnutrition, disease, drug and alcohol abuse, violence, injury, unplanned pregnancies enormously hamper human participation in development. |
| --- | --- | --- |
| | HIV/AIDS | Education promotes behavioural change for the disease undermines sustainable development by reducing participation of people, production of orphaned children who may not achieve their potentials, and contributing to missing teachers, and increased burden of care. |
| | Governance | Sustainable development is best promoted where governance structures enable transparency, expression of opinion, debate, input in policy formulation, and decision making. This framework promotes citizenry participation in setting parameters for sustainable development and good governance. |

| Ecological | Natural resources | ESD must continue to highlight the importance of the need to safeguard environmental resources as usually advocated in environmental education. Humanity depends on goods and services provided by ecosystems and their protection and restoration are sacrosanct. The link between societal and economic considerations should help promote behaviours necessary for protection and sparing use of resources. |
|---|---|---|
| | Climate change | ESD must inform learners of the link between poverty, economic development, and population growth to global warming and climate change and the effects of the later. |
| | Rural development | 60% of people in developing countries live in rural areas. Immense pressure is put on rural resources such as water, forests, soils leading to degradation and depletion, as well as other social issues such as poverty, lack of health facilities, schools and shelter. |
| | Sustainable urbanisation | Major towns and cities are riddled with slams and lack of infrastructure, health facilities, schools, shelter, jobs and food. These are threats to sustainable development. |
| | Disaster prevention and mitigation | Sustainable development is undermined where communities suffer disasters |

| | | or are threatened by them. Education for disaster risk reduction mitigates against this situation. |
|---|---|---|
| Economic | Poverty reduction | Poverty reduction increases the number of people contributing to sustainable development in terms of social, ecological and economic dimensions |
| | Corporate responsibility and accountability | Economic corporations influence political, economic and ecological improvements by mobilising resources both financial and human thus contributing to sustainable development. |
| | Market economy | Creation of global governance systems that are cognizant of ecological, political, social considerations contribute to sustainable development. |

## Teaching and Learning Experiences for ESD: Paradigm Shift in Education

ESD is for everyone and subscribes to lifelong learning, engaging all possible learning spaces, formal, non-formal and informal, from early childhood to adult life. The purpose is to enable the learner to adopt practices and behaviours which foster sustainable development, individually and collectively. In Israel and in several other countries ESD is considered as a part of life rather than just a subject in school.

The question we must answer is this: How do we get to sustainability? We can only get there if we have acquired requisite knowledge, skills, attitudes and values related to sustainability through ESD. Scholars in Israel and specifically at the David Yellin Academic College of Education in Jerusalem (the college is considered as the centre of excellence in ESD in Israel) including Eyal Bloch and Michal Yuval have outlined the **main values and principles in ESD** which include the following:

- **Authenticity**: Deal with what you really care about, be motivated by your Head, Hands, and Heart – i.e. combine knowledge, skills, and values in all your deeds;
- **Available resources**: Community, collaboration and respect; listen attentively and forget hierarchies. Every person can make a difference. Collaborate- work with people, and enjoy their spirit. Create a web of will, knowledge, experience and enthusiasm rather than look for "budget, stuff, and fossil energy. Monitor local resources and optimize their contribution. Share traditional knowledge, thoughts, ideas, and promote open source learning;
- **The Prosumer Approach**: Every child, citizen, a community member is both a producer and a consumer of knowledge, skills, values and customs;
- **Optimism, Creativity, and Humour:** In every problem hides its solution. Rethink, reconnect, recreate. Have fun;
- **Learning from Success Stories:** Whether traditional or futuristic, find out from colleagues and the web what solutions already exist;
- **Commitment:** Ask yourself, "what do I take upon myself to promote" rather than "what must/should/can be done by others"?; and
- **Revolutions and Evolution:** See the big picture (Revolution) and take small, effective steps (Evolution) where a relatively small effort will yield a big change.

ESD involves a paradigm shift in education in which we align our education systems with people and the Planet Earth; aligning it with sustainability. The drivers of this re-alignment are hope and transformative change. A paradigm shift occurs when a question is asked inside the current paradigm that can only be answered from outside it. The question must be genuine and leaves room for new and different questions to be raised as the initial question is explored, for the question not asked is a door not opened. When a question is properly asked it rivets our attention and all the creative power of our minds is focused on it. Knowledge emerges in response to the question, thus opening us up to new worlds. Think about these questions:

- What makes me alive?
- What makes me lively?
- What gives me energy?

To answer these questions you will search yourself for the answers rather than searching from other sources. You move from mere explanation to exploration. In essence, ESD provides opportunities for learners to open their minds, the process that is encouraged through the following activities and situations:

- Sharing as in group work;
- Sketching and graphic exploration;
- Improvement of existing information;
- Participation;
- Thinking, reflection and action; and
- Application of skill, emotion and knowledge.

The teacher ceases to be the owner of knowledge in the learning situation. Instead, the teacher becomes the leader of students, while the student acts as an innovator. The school should become the ESD centre and agent of change or what is sometimes referred to as "prosumers", while

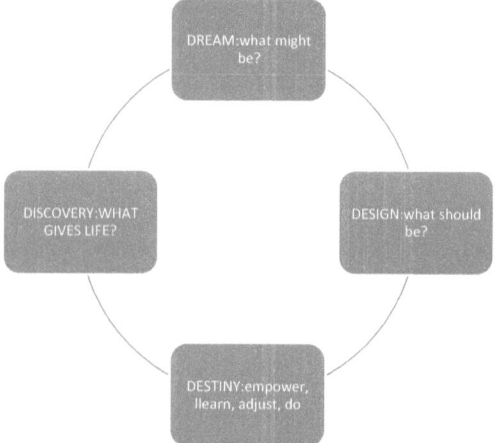

Figure 7.1: The Core Elements of Appreciative Pedagogy for ESD

the members of the community act as prosumers as well. This means that ESD students are involved in what can be referred to as "collapetition" whereby there are instances of collaboration, competition and cooperation among themselves and with teachers, members of the local communities among others.

The pedagogy preferred for ESD can be referred to as appreciative inquiry, which is summarised in Figure 7.1.

The outcome of this kind of pedagogy is the students' ability to understand:

- The significance of the commons; the traditions that direct our ways of life or the sense of connection (connectedness);

- The concept of interdependence; being apart and apart for a common cause; and
- Ecological literacy: Creating norms and actions relating to the natural environment.

This means that change begins with ourselves, but we must be given the tools to do so. Indeed a small group of committed people can change the world once they acquire the tools. The tools are the ability to decipher the commons, to act in the environment and to engage in critical thinking (Figure 7.2). The tools bring about the requisite transformative ESD.

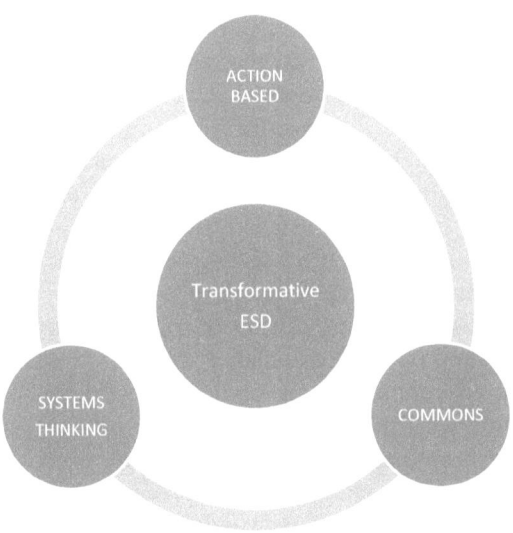

**Figure 7.2: Elements of Transformative Learning in ESD**

Thus ESD requires teachers to adopt novel skills and habits to generate the required change:

- **Set important goals**: Providing leadership and being skilful in teaching aimed at impacting on students for positive change with regard to sustainability;
- **Create powerful learning experiences**: Being creative and innovative such as the use of suitable medium (such as songs, poems, dance, graphics) to propagate powerful messages that help

nurture students' emotions and imagination and learning abilities;

- **Manage productive learning environments**: Use of local resources including learnscapes, Web 2.0, and ICT;
- **Know students**: Understand students' abilities, interests and learning styles;
- **Promote growth**: Encourage students to think "out of the box" and to use various sources of information. Including ICT;
- **Leverage teacher talent**: Act as a mediator between students and the teacher; and
- **Build community**: Promote cooperation and collaboration as a tool for building learning communities.

Thus ESD requires a re-examination of educational policy, in terms of re-orientation of education from nursery to university and continuing adult learning in order to focus more on the development of knowledge, skills, perspectives and values that promote sustainability. This implies a review of existing curricula in terms of their objectives, and content. This would help to develop trans-disciplinary understandings of social, economic, ecological and political sustainability. It also implies a review of the approaches to teaching, learning and assessment so that lifelong learning skills are fostered. These include skills for creative and critical thinking, oral and written communication, collaboration and cooperation, conflict management, decision-making, problem-solving and planning, using appropriate ICTs, and practical citizenship.

Overall, education systems need to be reviewed to promote the learning associated with sustainability. Teacher education would thus need to be appropriately packaged in order to prepare teachers for interactive learning processes, which encourage the development of values such as equity, dignity and respect which underpin sustainable development. Unnecessary competition promoted through drilling sidelines ingredients of sustainable development that are promoted through active learning, analytical thinking and critical appreciation of knowledge.

Education outside of the school in our daily life and interactions, at home and workplace, from the media, listening, reflection, observation should also contribute to the shaping of our practices and behaviours of sustainable development. Thus a re-orientation of the education system towards the principles and values of sustainable development eventually result in modelling in the classroom and by unselfconscious and widespread patterns of living and relating (UNESCO, 2006).

## Expected Outcomes of ESD

The following are some of the key outcomes of ESD initiatives:

- Broad public awareness of the nature and principles of sustainable development;
- Integration of educational components into plans for sustainable development;
- Assessment of the need for and role of ESD in all development planning;
- Developing consensus on the strategic importance of ESD;
- Understanding the thread of sustainable development woven into educational initiatives to improve the quality of education; and
- Adopting ESD-specific approaches in learning situations of all kinds

## ESD Stakeholders and their Roles and Strategies

Everyone is a stakeholder in ESD. All of us will feel the impact of its success or failure and all of us affect its impact on our behaviour. Complimentary roles and responsibilities radiate across the society and hence stakeholders include the government and intergovernmental bodies, international agencies and development partners, civil society, NGOs, the private sector, the media and advertising agents.

The roles and strategies employed by the stakeholders ensure that change in public attitudes and educational approaches keep pace with the evolving challenges of sustainable development. The outcomes of ESD will be seen in the lives of thousands of communities and millions of people as new attitudes and values inspire decisions and actions making sustainable development a more attainable ideal. The strategies include but not limited to the following:

- Advocacy and vision building;
- Consultation and ownership;
- Partnerships, alliances and networks;
- Capacity building and training;
- Research and innovation;
- Information and communication technologies; and
- Monitoring and evaluation

The government of Kenya and many other countries throughout the world have taken important steps to implement ESD in the education system and among the citizens outside the education system. The mandate for this purpose has been bestowed to the Ministry of Education and the National Environment Management Authority (NEMA). The impetus for progress in ESD has been provided by various legal provisions. Section 42(4) of the Basic Education Act, 2013 directs the Cabinet Secretary for education in Kenya to promote environmental protection through education for sustainable development (ESD). The National ESD policy was adopted by parliament in 2015 and commits all institutions to implement ESD. The SDG 4 ensures that inclusive and equitable quality education is provided that promote lifelong opportunities. Target 2 commits governments to ensure that by 2030 all learners acquire the knowledge and skills needed to promote sustainable development including through ESD and sustainable lifestyles, human rights, gender equality, promotion of a culture of peace and non-violence, global citizenship and appreciation of cultural diversity and of cultures contribution to sustainable development. Finally, Resolution 37 C(12) endorsed by UNESCO 37TH General Conference held in November 2013 upholds the Global Action Programme as the follow-up to the UN Decade of Education for Sustainable Development (see Ndaruga, 2014; NEMA, 2008; NEMA, 2013; UNESCO, 2004 and 2006).

The following are some of the key steps that have been taken to implement ESD:

- Development of ESD implementation strategy (2005-2014) by NEMA in collaboration with other stakeholders;
- The Ministry of Education has entered into a longtime collaboration with the State of Israel for the purpose of capacity building in ESD. Teachers and university lecturers have been trained in the dynamics of ESD since 2012;
- Encouraging every sector of the economy to mainstream ESD in their activities; through the development of specific sector ESD strategies;
- NEMA has developed environmental education resource materials to sensitise various stakeholders on ESD e.g. booklets, brochures, posters, stickers, magazines and e-books with a specific message relevant to events and occasions; and
- Establishing modalities by NEMA for public participation in environmental management activities; with sustainability in mind; these include:

- Collaboration with civil society organisation;
- Collaboration with media on diverse topics resulting in the publication of articles, supplements, talk shows documentaries in both print and electronic media;
- Partnership with the private sector, in activities such as clean-ups, and support for events such as World Environment Day (WED); and
- Gazettement of environmental inspectors, who help in ensuring compliance with environmental standards.

## Summary

You have learned that ESD is the type of education that seeks to integrate the key values inherent in sustainable development, espoused in the various documents such as the Earth Charter and Caring for the Earth, into all aspects of learning to encourage changes in behaviour that allow more sustainable living. ESD is a precursor to environmental education for sustainability; every effort should be made to understand its basic structure and philosophy as a basis for environmental educational for sustainability.

Education for sustainable development should not be equated with environmental education. The latter is a well-established discipline, which focuses on humankind's relationship with the natural environment and on ways to conserve and preserve it and properly steward its resources. Sustainable development therefore encompasses environmental education, setting it in the broader context of socio-cultural factors and the socio-political issues of equity, poverty, democracy and quality of life.

The government of Kenya, and many other countries throughout the world, has taken important steps to implement ESD in the education system and among the citizens outside the education system. The mandate for this purpose has been bestowed to the Ministry of Education and the National Environment Management Authority (NEMA), (Ndaruga, 2014).

## End of Chapter Activities

- How is ESD related to environmental education for sustainability?
- In Israel, ESD is considered as part of life rather than a subject for learning in school. Explain?
- Explain the content and learning experiences for ESD?
- Explain the strategies being used to implement ESD in Kenya?
- One renown educator said: "The longest distance on Earth is the 3cm length between the head and the heart". Discuss this

statement in light of ESD implementation.

## Bibliography

Australian Government (2005)
    Educating for a Sustainable Future: A National Environmental
    Education Statement for Australian Schools. Carlton South:
    Commonwealth of Australia
Australian Government (2007)
    Caring for Our Future: The Australian Government Strategy for
    the United Nations Decade of Education for Sustainable
    Development, 2005-2014. Canberra : Commonwealth of Australia
Commonwealth of Australia (2000)
    Environmental Education for a Sustainable Future: A National
    Action Plan. Canberra: Environment Education Unit
NEMA (2008).
    Education for Sustainable Development: .Implementation Strategy.
    Nairobi: NEMA
NEMA (2013).
    Education for Sustainable Development-Kenya Report, 2012.
    Nairobi: NEMA
Ndaruga, Ayub Macharia (2014)
    ESD Explained. Nairobi: TECHlEARN Institute
    (https://play.google.com/store/apps/details?id+captain.ayub.esd.
    AOVOOCCJHLBFBQMN)
Tilbury, D(1995).
    Environmental Education for Sustainability. Developing the New
    focus of Environmental Education in the 1990s.Environmental
    Education Research 1(2), 195-212
UNESCO (2006)
    Framework for the United Nations Decade of Education for
    Sustainable Development (UNDESD) International
    Implementation Scheme. Paris: Unesco

# 8

## CHAPTER 8

# FROM ENVIRONMENTAL EDUCATION TO EDUCATION FOR SUSTAINABILITY

## Introduction

Environmental Education (EE) as we know it today has been riddled with some fundamental weaknesses in scope and pedagogy. The pedagogical approaches used have been narrow in scope and failed to promote an understanding of the complexity of the world in which we live and the knowledge, critical thinking skills, values and capacity to participate in decision making about environmental and development issues. There is every need for schools and other institutions to prepare and empower learners to assume responsibility for creating and enjoying a sustainable future. We need a transformative education that benefits from creative and innovative teaching and learning. Environmental Education for sustainability is a new approach to teaching and learning about the environment and builds on the dynamics of Education for Sustainable Development. This chapter outlines the significance of Environmental Education for Sustainability as a new type of transformative education aimed at helping learners to attain sustainable living.

## Meaning of Environmental Education for Sustainability

At the time when the United Nations Conference on the Human Environment was held in Stockholm in 1972, the environment was seen primarily as a set of natural ecosystems and values with the environmental crisis coming from problems such as the increasing pollution of land, air and water, growth of the world's population and the continuing depletion of natural resources.

Ideas about Environmental Education continued to evolve during the 1970s and by 1977 at the Tbilisi conference the goals, objectives, and guiding principles were formulated. These have underpinned much of what happened in the name of EE in many countries of the world.

The guiding principles of EE have emphasised considerations of the environment in its totality - natural and cultural, technological and social. This holistic approach to the environment was a major shift from programmes that hitherto focused only on the natural environment and thus failed to understand the role of human decisions and actions in causing ecological problems.

During the 1980s and 1990s, the use of the language of sustainable development, or simply as sustainability, began to emerge, popularised by the World Commission on Environment and Development in 1987(Brundtland Commission) and revisited in 1992 through the United Nations Conference on Environment and Development in Rio de Janeiro. Since that time a much stronger emphasis has been placed upon trying to integrate thinking and action around *ecological, social, political and economic systems* as being critical to achieving sustainable future.

In 2002, the World Summit on Sustainable Development confirmed this relationship in declaring education for sustainability as critical for promoting sustainable development. According to Agenda 21:

*Education is critical for achieving environmental and ethical awareness, values and attitudes, skills and behaviour consistent with sustainable development and for effective public participation in decision making.*

Sustainable development can only be achieved where people are well-informed of the challenges and have the relevant knowledge, skills and motivation to address them. The United Nations Decade of Education for Sustainable Development (UNDESD) was therefore declared at the summit covering the period 2005-2014. The decade identifies the role of education as a critical tool in our efforts to achieve more ecologically, economically, politically and socially sustainable development. Societies around the world were urged to begin re-orienting their education systems towards sustainability during the period.

Environmental education for sustainability focuses on all components that impact on the environment, namely, social, ecological, economic, and political dimensions. This new look at environmental education is influenced by "Education for Sustainable Development" that is viewed as a life-wide and lifelong endeavour which challenges individuals, institutions and societies to view tomorrow as a day that belongs to all of us, or it will not belong to anyone (United Nations Decade for Sustainable Development 2005 - 2014).

Education for sustainability introduces a focus on values and ethics and on new challenges for multi-disciplinary and inter-disciplinary dialogue, teaching and research. The aim is to promote future thinking, lifelong learning and capacity building for individual and organisation change; to better equip the society to take informed actions towards sustainable development.

Following the UNDESD declaration, Environmental Education has now evolved in the 21st century to embody sustainability in the broadest sense. Environmental Education for sustainability is a concept encompassing a vision of education that seeks to empower people of all ages to assume responsibility for creating a sustainable future; by trying to integrate thinking and action around *ecological, social, political and economic systems* as being critical to achieving sustainable future; and by establishing an ethic of caring towards the environment. Its emphasis is on *transformational change* in values and behaviour from the individual to a global scale.

## Milestones in the Evolution of the Concept of Sustainable Development

The concept of sustainable development emerged in the 1980s in response to a growing realisation of the need to balance economic and social progress with concern for the environment and the stewardship of natural resources. The following are the major milestones in the evolution of the concept.

- The 1972 United Nations Conference on the Human Environment held in Stockholm placed environmental issues on the international political agenda for the first time. It promoted the importance of environmental issues at a national level and encouraged the development of national policies and the creation of many environmental ministries and non-governmental organisations (NGOs) working to conserve the environment. It also gave birth to the establishment of the United Nations Environmental Programme (UNEP) and the Convention on International Trade of Endangered Species (CITES);

- The concept of sustainable development gained worldwide support with the publication of *Our Common Future* by the World Commission on Environment and Development in 1987. The Commission defined sustainable development as 'development that meets the needs of the present without compromising the ability of future generations to meet their own needs'. This definition stresses that while development is necessary to improve the quality of human life, the capacity of the natural resource base should not be impaired;

- The United Nations Conference on Environment and Development (UNCED) (Earth Summit) held in Rio de Janeiro in 1992 established the fundamental principle that economic development can and must go hand in hand with environmental protection. It suggested that economic, social and environmental considerations were intertwined with issues of poverty, equity, quality of life, and global environmental protection. It adopted Agenda 21, a framework for action at national and international levels to assist governments and other institutions in implementing sustainable development policies and programmes. The Rio Declaration was signed showing a commitment to a 'global partnership to conserve, protect and restore the health and integrity of the Earth's ecosystem'. The United Nations Commission on Sustainable Development was created to ensure follow-up of UNCED while UNESCO was tasked with the development and implementation of Education for Sustainable Development (ESD);

- A follow-up discussion on Agenda 21 (chapter 36 on Education, Public Awareness and Training) was done at the International Conference on Environment and Society held in Thessaloniki, Greece in December 1997 under the auspices of UNESCO. It focused on the role of environmental education and public awareness in fostering sustainable development. It was realised that in order to achieve sustainability, enormous coordination and integration of efforts are required in various sectors and rapid and radical change of behaviours and lifestyles, including changing consumption and production patterns. The idea of education for sustainability was recognised as a pillar of sustainable development together with legislation, economy and technology and a proposal for the establishment of a conceptual framework for Education for Sustainability (ESD) within the context of environmental education;

- In the year 2000, the Earth Charter was launched at The Hague, Netherlands. This was a civil call for sustainability and a declaration of fundamental principles for building a just, sustainable and peaceful society in the 21$^{st}$ century, based on respect for nature, diversity, universal human rights, economic justice and a culture of peace. The charter sets forth a concise formulation of the meaning of sustainable living and development. The Charter provides an elaboration of sustainable development in terms of ecological, social, political, and economic dimensions. The participants in implementing the charter should include students, governments, leaders, local authorities, communities and international agencies. It is a living charter with the power to unite people for a common purpose: care and concern for the whole community, including the environment;
- The International Conference on Financing for Development held in Monterrey, Mexico, in 2002, established the basis for the financing of sustainable development activities; and
- The World Summit on Sustainable Development (WSSD) was then held in Johannesburg in 2002 to enhance the implementation of the resolutions on sustainable development by governments. The political Declaration at the summit states that sustainable development is built on three mutually reinforcing pillars-economic development, social development and environmental protection - which must be established at local, national, and levels. Practical ways to achieve progress in sustainable development were examined including increased access to basic requirements such as clean water, sanitation, adequate shelter, energy, healthcare, food security, and the protection of biodiversity. This is to be achieved through increasing access to funding and opening of markets, capacity building, the use of modern technology and the formation of stronger regional partnerships. The summit also sought ways for fighting against vices such as diseases, and to empower women and emancipate indigenous people to ensure that all participate in sustainable development.

To provide the momentum for this, the United Nations Decade of Education for Sustainable Development (UNDESD) was declared to cover the period 2005 - 2014. Environmental Education for sustainability is now the agenda for education at all levels and across all sectors. The 4$^{th}$ International Conference on Environment Education held in Ahmadabad, India, in 2007 provided further momentum on the achievement of sustainable development through the provisions of UNDESD.

## Expected Outcomes of Environmental Education for Sustainability (EES)

The goal of EES is to provide learners with an understanding of, and concern for, stewardship of the natural environment, and the knowledge to contribute to ecologically sustainable development (Australian Government, 2005).

The goal entails the following specific objectives:

- Providing skills in analysis and problem-solving and the ability to communicate ideas and information and to collaborate with others.
- Providing the capacity to exercise judgment and responsibility in matters of morality, ethics and social justice, and the capacity to make sense of their world, to think about how things got to be the way they are, to make rational and informed decisions about their own lives, and to accept responsibility for their own actions.
- Providing an understanding and appreciation of their system of government and civic life so that they can be active and informed citizens
- Providing the knowledge, skills and attitudes necessary to establish and maintain a healthy lifestyle and for the creative and satisfying use of leisure time.

Environmental Education for Sustainability is, therefore, a concept encompassing a vision of education that seeks to empower people of all ages to assume responsibility for creating a sustainable future (UNESCO, 2004). This is possible since EES seeks to promote an understanding of the complexity of the world in which we live and the knowledge, critical thinking skills, values and capacity to participate in decision making about environmental and development issues. Through EES schools and other institutions are expected to prepare and empower learners to assume responsibility for creating and enjoying a sustainable future. EES is therefore expected to be a transformative education that benefits from creative and innovative teaching and learning.

Box 8.1

Discussion

Are you able to note that ESS is a continual modification of EE to make the later more relevant in the 21st century when sustainability in our lives is a rule rather than an exception and a fundamental driver in making pedagogical decisions? It is certain that in the 21st-century environmental education has changed and now embodies sustainability with an emphasis on transformational change in values and behaviour from the individual to a global scale.

## Summary

In this chapter, you have learned that Environmental Education as we know it today has not provided the transformative education that benefits from creative and innovative teaching and learning. Environmental Education for sustainability is currently a new approach to teaching and learning about the environment and builds on the dynamics of Education for Sustainable Development. Environmental Education for Sustainability is, therefore, a concept encompassing a vision of education that seeks to empower people of all ages to assume responsibility for creating a sustainable future. This is possible since EES seeks to promote an understanding of the complexity of the world in which we live and the knowledge, critical thinking skills, values and capacity to participate in decision making about environmental and development issues. Through EES schools and other institutions are expected to prepare and empower learners to assume responsibility for creating and enjoying a sustainable future.

## End of Chapter Activities

- Differentiate between Environmental Education and Environmental Education for Sustainability?
- Provide reasons for the paradigm shift in the provision of environmental education in the 21st century.
- Explain the influence of ESD in the transformation of Environmental Education to Environmental Education for

Sustainability?

## Bibliography

Australian Government (2005)
>Educating for a Sustainable Future: A National Environmental Education Statement for Australian Schools. Carlton South: Commonwealth of Australia

Australian Government (2007)
>Caring for Our Future: The Australian Government Strategy for the United Nations Decade of Education for Sustainable Development, 2005-2014. Canberra: Commonwealth of Australia

Commonwealth of Australia (2000)
>Environmental Education for a Sustainable Future: A National Action Plan. Canberra: Environment Education Unit

UNESCO (2004)
>United Nations Decade of Education for Sustainable Development 2005-2014. Paris: UNESCO

UNESCO (2006)
>Framework for the United Nations Decade of Education for Sustainable Development (UNDESD) International Implementation Scheme. Paris: Unesco

# 9

## CHAPTER 9

## FRAMEWORK FOR IMPLEMENTATION OF ENVIRONMENTAL EDUCATION FOR SUSTAINABILITY

### Introduction

This chapter introduces the concept of environmental education for sustainability in the school curriculum. It outlines how environmental education for sustainability in schools can be planned for and organised to achieve the learning objectives. You will be able to understand that environmental education for sustainability is a core feature of the value structure of the school (school ethos) and should be reflected in the whole school operations. You will also learn that implementing environmental education for sustainability in schools requires the development of a shared vision, goals and objectives as provided for in a framework for environmental education for sustainability (Australian Government, 2005).

**Expected Learning Outlines**

By the end of this chapter you should be able to:

- Demonstrate the ability to state the school vision for the development and implementation of environmental education for sustainability;
- Demonstrate the ability to develop the goals and objectives of environmental education for sustainability that schools should set to achieve;
- Demonstrate an understanding of the difference between the goals and objectives of environmental education and those for environmental education for sustainability;
- Discuss the extent environmental education for sustainability is a core feature of the value structure of the school (school ethos); and
- Discuss the factors that lead to the successful implementation of environmental education for sustainability within the school framework.

## Environmental Education for Sustainability: The Whole School Approach

Effective environmental education for sustainability requires the involvement of the **whole school,** sometimes referred to as the **Whole School Approach** to environmental education. It cuts across all aspects of the school operations: curriculum; teaching and learning; physical surroundings; and relations with the local community. All the groups that make up a school community are involved: the administration staff, the teaching staff, the grounds staff, the canteen staff, the parents, the students and the local community. It is best observed in how the school administration, teachers, students, parents, the surrounding community and other stakeholders interrelate in supporting the school's programmes to promote sustainability.

Students from Milton Hershey School working on a landscaping project. Photo/TOM CHERRY

Developing and implementing environmental education for sustainability, therefore, requires the school to develop an elaborate and clear shared vision, goals and objectives. The school vision guides and directs decisions on how the school is organised and the roles assumed by the school administration, teachers, students, parents, the community and other stakeholders. It is, therefore, an important component of the whole school approach to environmental education for sustainability. The vision also informs the goals and objectives of environmental education for sustainability. As a teacher of environmental education for sustainability, you will be required to help your school develop a vision that will help it develop the learning experiences and provide the support that will ensure the objectives of environmental education for sustainability are achieved.

According to Australian Government (2005) it is envisioned that: *The school is a legal and dynamic organization where creative and reflective thinking and actions, as well as evaluation of these, are valued and sustainability and community are central to all operations; The school administration is supportive and actively involved in environmental education for sustainability initiatives; The teachers are resigned to effectively plan and teach to attain the goals and objectives of environmental education for sustainability; and the students are active participants and self-directed learners capable of ethical and responsible actions in the environment.*

# Goals and Objectives of Environmental Education for Sustainability

Effective environmental education for sustainability curriculum provides the knowledge and understandings, skills, attitudes, and values, and opportunities for participation and action that will help students to create a sustainable future. These attributes have to be identified and the goals and objectives clearly stated.

## Goals

The goals of environmental education for sustainability are to develop the capacities of students to:

- Understand and value the interdependence of social, cultural, economic, and ecological dimensions at local, national, and global levels;
- Reflect critically upon how this interdependence affects communities, workplaces, families and individuals and be able to make appropriate decisions;
- Develop attitudes and skills which are conducive to the achievement of a sustainable future;
- Appreciate and respect the intrinsic value of the whole environment and a sense of the sacred;
- Develop an ethic of personal responsibility and stewardship towards all aspects of the environment; and
- Participate as active and involved citizens in building a sustainable future.

## Objectives

Schools will have to plan learning activities that enable students to achieve the following objectives:

a) Knowledge and Understandings:

- To explain the nature and function of ecological, social, economic, and political systems and how they are interrelated;
- To identify the natural and cultural values intrinsic to the environment;
- To analyse the impact of people on the environment and how the

environment shapes human activities, with particular reference to Kenya's environment;

- To establish the ways different cultures view the importance of sacredness in the environment;
- To determine the role of cultural, socioeconomic and political systems in environmental decision making;
- To outline the principles of ecologically sustainable development;
- To identify the responsibilities and benefits of environmental citizenship, including the conservation and protection of environmental values;
- To identify the importance of respecting and conserving indigenous knowledge and cultural heritage; and
- To explain how knowledge is uncertain and may change over time and why we, therefore, need to exercise caution in all our interactions with the environment.

b) Skills and capabilities

The students should develop the ability to engage in:

- Explorations of the many dimensions of the environment using all of their senses;
- Observations and recording of information, ideas and feelings about the environment;
- Identification and assessment of environmental issues;
- Critical and creative thinking about environmental challenges and opportunities;
- Consideration and prediction of the consequences of environmental actions (social, cultural, economic, and ecological);
- Oral, written and graphic communication of environmental issues and solutions to others;
- Cooperation and negotiation to resolve conflicts that arise over environmental issues; and
- Individual and collective action to support desirable outcomes.

c) Attitudes and Values

The students should be able to show an appreciation and commitment to:

- Respecting and caring for life in all its diversity;
- Conserving and managing resources in ways that are fair to present

and future generations;

- Building democratic societies that are just, sustainable, participatory and peaceful, and
- Understanding and conserving cultural heritage.

d) Action and Participation

Students should be able to apply knowledge and understandings, skills, attitudes and values in active and informed participation to address environmental issues, problems and opportunities by displaying:

- A willingness to examine and change personal lifestyles to secure a sustainable future;
- The ability to identify, investigate, evaluate and undertake appropriate action to maintain, protect and enhance local and global environments;
- A willingness to challenge preconceived ideas, accept change and acknowledge uncertainty; and
- The ability to work cooperatively and in partnership with others.

## Implementation of Whole - School Approach to Environmental Education for Sustainability

Effective environmental education for sustainability requires the involvement of the whole school. It cuts across all aspects of the school operations: curriculum; teaching and learning; physical surroundings; and relations with the local community. All the groups that make up a school community are involved: the administration staff, the teaching staff, the grounds staff, the canteen staff, the parents, the students and the local community.

The key way to implement environmental education for sustainability in the curriculum, therefore, involves a whole-school approach, working across all curriculum areas and complemented by whole-school policies and activities in other related areas. This requires the adoption of a clear value structure of the school or school ethos, including the organisation of teaching and learning, school governance, physical surrounds, resource management, curriculum organisation, and networks and partnerships formed (Australian Government, 2005). This then forms the basis for the development of a shared vision, goals, and objectives to drive the whole-school approach initiative with regard to environmental management.

The impact of the whole-school approach is, therefore, best

observed in how administrators, teachers, students, parents and community interrelate with respect to environmental management; in programmes offered to students; and how the school embraces the principles of good citizenship in the way it operates as a learning community. It involves:

- How the school is organised and operates (*Governance*);
- Development and management of school grounds as well as school design (*Physical surrounds*);
- Reduction and minimisation of resource (water, energy, products and materials) use by the school as well as conservation and protection of heritage values in the school and its grounds (*Resource management*);
- Enhanced connections between the school, its community and other educational institutions (*Networks and partnerships*); and
- Reorientation of the curriculum and the teaching and learning towards sustainability (*Curriculum organisation and teaching and learning).*

## Success factors in the Whole School Approach

- Active participation of the school leadership at all stages of the programme;
- Clear vision and mission based on the goals and aspirations of environmental education for sustainability;
- Sustainability principles incorporated in school policies and practices;
- An implementation team is drawn from all divisions of the school guided by clear terms of reference and timelines;
- A clear view of the school operations and state of the environment prior to moving into action;
- Providing information on the progress of the work and celebrating the successes; and
- Established learnscapes where a learning programme is designed to permit students to interact with the environment (Australian Government, 2005). This may involve increasing the diversity of school grounds and buildings by adding features such as flower beds, gardens, forests, ponds, outdoor classrooms among others that provide opportunities for interaction and learning experiences.

Box 9.1

## Discussion

### The Eco School and the ESD Initiatives

Some selected schools in Kenya under the Eco school and ESD initiatives integrate environmental education into a holistic program with measurable environmental, economic, social, governance and curriculum outcomes. The initiatives implement efficiencies in a school's management of resources such as energy, waste, and water and the management of school grounds such as biodiversity, landscaping, and soil conservation. The schools integrate these in teaching and learning in the school curriculum. The enterprise involves members of the community, all members of the school and sponsors. The schools apply the whole-school approach to environmental education as a key step in fulfilling the ideals of environmental education for sustainability.

### School Governance

Schools are expected to prepare students to take their role as useful members of society after school. Good governance involves allowing students to participate in decision making in important school matters. This helps them to maximise their use of resources in a socially, ecologically, and economically sustainable way. In this process, students gain the skills and values useful for application in their day to day lives even after school.

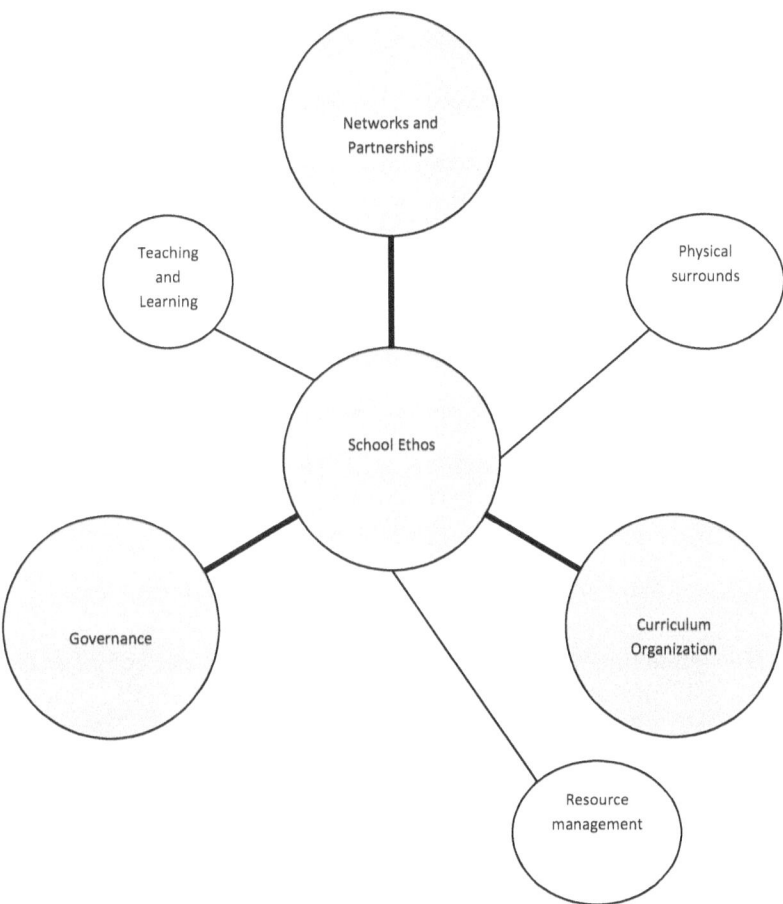

Figure 9.1: Components of the Whole School Approach to Environmental Education for Sustainability

## Resource Management

Schools are expected to be sustainable organisations. This should be reflected in their daily operations. To achieve this, the schools should commit their resources, both financial and human to identifying, conserving, and improving the environmental and heritage values of the schools and by reducing their ecological footprint. This could be done progressively by reducing waste through more recycling and use of fewer materials; minimising the use of energy, water and transport; encouraging biodiversity in the school grounds; conserving the heritage value of the school; using sound purchasing practices, and ensuring canteen products are environmentally appropriate. Overall, savings will be made which could be used for other sustainability activities.

## Physical Surrounds

The school ambience results from the physical appearance and presentation of the grounds and buildings. The schools may be limited in terms of the design of the existing buildings, but the refurbishing of the older buildings as well as the new ones should embrace energy saving mechanisms. However, sustainable management of the grounds through activities such as habitat creation, mulching, appropriate vegetable gardening, landscaping, litter binning, improving grass lawns, flower beds and hedges, and increasing diversity and extent of vegetation cover in the school grounds enhance the image of the school grounds as well as providing opportunities for outdoor education. Students, staff, parents and community members can be encouraged to be actively involved in these sustainable management activities.

## Networks and Partnerships

Many important environmental education initiatives can be undertaken and achieved through collaborative initiatives with local, national and international agencies including other educational institutions, local government authorities, businesses, industry, and community groups and networks. This links students' learning to the workplace and to local environmental and social issues. In this process, students are allowed access to financial resources and information otherwise not available to the school and also to interact with skilled personnel.

From these collaborative initiatives, students should be allowed to create the schools' cultural and social heritage by researching and documenting the history of the school and its links with the community and by setting up the heritage as well as caring for it.

## Curriculum Organisation

Environmental education for sustainability curriculum involves all the attributes of the school including the structured learning activities. All these attributes should be organized in such a way that students' engagement is increased through practical learning experiences, often outside the boundaries of the classroom. The focus should be on helping them understand the present environment: how it has been shaped, the value in which it is held, and mitigation of adverse effects on it. This involves an investigation of how this situation has been reached and accepting responsibility to work towards a sustainable future. Identifying what is distinctive about the local environment and understanding local community issues is essential to shaping the environmental education programmes in schools.

The organisation of environmental education for sustainability can take many forms including the following key ones:

- Integrating environmental education for sustainability issues and topics into specific key learning areas or subjects such as languages, history and government, geography, mathematics, biology, chemistry, physics and business studies;
- Having a separate subject such as environmental science, environmental studies or environmental education; and
- Developing environmental education for sustainability issues or themes as cross-curricular units to be taught either by one teacher or several teachers in a collaborative approach.

## Teaching and Learning

The major purpose of environmental education for sustainability is to empower students to create a sustainable future. This is done by helping them to develop a better understanding of the world in which we live and providing them opportunities to develop the skills and values necessary for participation in actions that improve the quality of the environment. In this setup, the teaching and learning approaches will need to provide opportunities for the students to engage in problem-solving, teamwork, decision making, holistic thinking, clarifying and analysing values, and environmental action and participation.

## Indicators of a Sustainable School

Some indicators are essential as assessment guidelines for the sustainability of institutions such as schools. The essential indicators as adopted from the Australian Government (2005) are summarised in Table 9.1.

**Table 9.1: Indicators for a Sustainable School**

| ASPECT OF CHANGE FOR SUSTAINABILITY | INDICATOR |
|---|---|
| Educational | -The extent to which the school staff has participated in professional development in environmental education<br>-The extent to which all staff |

| | |
|---|---|
| | members have participated in professional development activities to gain an understanding of Ecological Sustainable Development (ESD) -Whether the school curriculum supports the principles of environmental education -The extent to which the school community has been educated to actively participate in the sustainable management of the school. |
| Environmental | -Whether the objectives of the school's overarching management plans and/or policies explicitly mention ESD -Whether the school has a school environmental management plan (SEMP) -Whether the school is implementing the SEMP -The extent to which the plan incorporates a long-term vision for the school in its move towards sustainability -The extent to which the school considers the environmental consequences of its actions, for example when purchasing products, or during construction or demolition - The extent to which there is support from other levels of the education system to assist the school achieve sustainability such as facilities and operations sections -Whether an environmental audit has been completed to collect baseline data. |
| Economic | -The extent of savings from a baseline or previous year of reduction of waste to landfill -The extent of savings from a baseline or previous year of reduction of energy use |

| | |
|---|---|
| | - The extent of savings from a baseline or previous year of reduction of water consumption<br>- The extent to which commercial enterprises in the school support the SEMP<br>-Whether the school has attracted additional funds from sponsorships and other sources. |
| Water resources | -The extent to which water consumption at baseline date and since participating in the initiative has been reduced in KL per annum<br>- The extent to which factors may have influenced the results (e.g. a leaking pipe, reduction strategies implemented, not targeted in SEMP and other). |
| Electricity | -The extent to which electricity consumption at baseline date and since participating in the initiative has been reduced in Kilowatt hours per annum<br>- The extent to which factors may have influenced the results (e.g. a heat wave, reduction strategies implemented, not targeted in SEMP and other). |
| Waste | - The extent to which waste to landfill (from the audit and bills) at baseline date and since participating in the initiative has been reduced by the number of bins<br>- The extent to which factors may have influenced the results (e.g. construction, reduction strategies implemented, not targeted in SEMP and other). |
| School grounds | - The extent to which the school has increased the variety of habitats in the school ground<br>-The extent to which factors may have influenced the results (e.g. projects |

| | undertaken, drought, construction, reduction strategies implemented, not targeted in SEMP and other) <br> -Whether the school grounds contain local indigenous vegetation <br> -The extent to which the area of indigenous vegetation has increased since participating in the initiative <br> -Whether landscape design reduces the consumption of resources(e.g. shade trees planted near buildings, mulch added, or drip irrigation installed) |
|---|---|
| Social | -The extent to which partnerships have been established between the school and the local community (e.g. environmental experts, local businesses, government and non-governmental organisations) <br> -The extent to which the school community is active in the development and implementation of the SEMP <br> - The extent to which the local community is actively participating in the development and implementation of the SEMP <br> - The extent to which the school community has shifted towards more sustainable practices and processes <br> - The extent to which the school has encouraged the broader community to shift towards more sustainable practices and processes. |

## Summary

This chapter has introduced the concept of environmental education for sustainability in the school curriculum. It has outlined how environmental education for sustainability in schools can be planned for and organized to achieve the learning objectives. It has shown that environmental education for sustainability is a core feature of the value structure of the school (school ethos) and should be reflected in the whole school operations, including school governance, use of resources, partnerships and networks, among others.

You also learned that implementing environmental education for sustainability in schools requires the development of a shared vision, goals and objectives as provided for in a framework for environmental education for sustainability. Some selected schools in Kenya under the green school and ESD initiatives integrate environmental education into a holistic program with measurable environmental, economic, social, governance and curriculum outcomes. The initiatives implement efficiencies in a school's management of resources such as energy, waste, and water and the management of school grounds such as biodiversity, landscaping, and soil conservation. The schools integrate these in teaching and learning in the school curriculum. The enterprise involves members of the community, all members of the school and sponsors. The schools apply the whole-school approach to environmental education as a key step in fulfilling the ideals of environmental education for sustainability.

## End of Chapter Activities

- Explain the components necessary for the implementation of environmental education for sustainability?
- Outline the components of the whole school approach necessary for the implementation of environmental education for sustainability?
- How are the green school and ESD initiatives in Kenya promoting environmental education for sustainability?

## Bibliography

Australian Government (2005)
    Educating for a Sustainable Future: A National Environmental Education Statement for Australian Schools. Carlton South: Commonwealth of Australia
Australian Government (2007)
    Caring for Our Future: The Australian Government Strategy for the United Nations Decade of Education for Sustainable Development, 2005-2014. Canberra: Commonwealth of Australia
Commonwealth of Australia (2000)
    Environmental Education for a Sustainable Future: A National Action Plan. Canberra: Environment Education Unit

# 10

## CHAPTER 10

## CURRICULUM IN ENVIRONMENTAL EDUCATION FOR SUSTAINABILITY

### Introduction

Environmental education for sustainability curriculum involves understanding the present environment (how it has been shaped, the value in which it's held, and seeking to mitigate adverse effects on it). This involves an exploration of the local environment to understand how we have come to this state and accepting responsibility to work towards a sustainable future. This approach helps to understand the local community's environmental issues and the role of the school in mitigating the issues. With this background information, the curriculum is then modelled to increase students' engagement through relevant practical activities mainly outside the classroom while taking account of their lives and interests.

This chapter outlines how environmental education for sustainability can be developed, organised and implemented in such a manner that learners are provided practical learning opportunities to fully participate in sustainable development. You will be able to understand how environmental education is incorporated into the school curriculum and the approaches used in teaching environmental education from a sustainability perspective.

**Expected Learning Outcomes**

By the end of this topic you should be able to:

- Outline and discuss the specific elements of the major components of environmental education for sustainability curriculum;
- Discuss the main ways in which the content of environmental education for sustainability is incorporated in the secondary school curriculum;
- Construct a school-based curriculum in environmental education for sustainability for the purpose of teaching through the regular school curriculum;
- Examine the methods, techniques and strategies of teaching environmental education for sustainability in the school curriculum;
- Plan and teach lessons in the curriculum within the framework of environmental education for sustainability; and
- Discuss the factors affecting the successful implementation of environmental education for sustainability in the secondary schools of Kenya.

## Content of Environmental Education for Sustainability Curriculum in Secondary Schools

Consistent with the goals, objectives, guiding principles and structure of environmental education outlined earlier in this module, any programme in environmental education for sustainability should consist of cognitive and affective components that enable learners to develop the requisite environmental knowledge and understanding, skills, attitudes and values. The components have been developed over the years largely through the efforts of the International Environmental Education Programme (IEEP), UNESCO and UNEP. There are presently four levels of cognitive knowledge and skills that any programme in environmental education for sustainability should include, namely:

- Key concepts and themes of education for sustainability;
- Key concepts and principles of environmental education for sustainability(conceptual awareness);
- Environmental investigation skills; and
- Environmental participation and action skills.

## Key Concepts and Themes of Education for Sustainability

These are the concepts and principles related to each of the four UNESCO systems of sustainability that provide the learner with sufficient ecological, social, political and economic sustainability knowledge to permit him or her to understand the need for sustainability and to make sustainably sound decisions (Table 10.1). The goal is to help students to participate in protecting and restoring the integrity of earth's ecological systems, with special concern for biological diversity and the natural processes that sustain life (ecological sustainability).

**Table 10.1: Key Concepts and Themes of Education for Sustainability**

| Ecological Sustainability | Social Sustainability | Economic Sustainability | Political Sustainability |
|---|---|---|---|
| Biodiversity/sacredness of nature | Basic human needs | Cost-benefit analysis | Citizenship |
| Habitat | Cultural diversity | Economic development | Democracy |
| Carrying capacity | Cultural heritage | Economic growth | Decision making |
| Conservation | Human rights | Eco-efficiency | Tolerance |
| Ecological footprint | Intergenerational equity | Life-cycle analysis | Power |
| Ecology | Participation | Natural capital | Respect |
| Eco space | Peace | Natural resource accounting | Conflict resolution |
| Ecosystems | Risk management | Steady-state economy | |
| Interspecies equity | Social justice | Sustainable consumption | |
| Natural cycles and systems | Equality | Sustainable production | |

| Appropriate technology | | Triple bottom line | |
|---|---|---|---|
| Life support systems | | Appropriate development | |
| Energy transfer | | | |

The concepts include, but not limited to, the following: Biodiversity, habitat, carrying capacity, conservation, ecological footprint, ecosystems, ecospace, interspecies equity, natural cycles and systems. An elaboration of these concepts is outlined below.

## Organisational levels in nature

- Three distinct levels of being exist: human, biological, and physical;
- The physical planet, its atmosphere, and lithosphere all obey physical laws and forces of change;
- The biological system (individuals, populations, communities) shows profound diversity (**biodiversity**);
- All environmental systems show variation in several forms - biological, cultural, social and economic. We need to understand the importance and value of each of these forms of diversity to the quality of human life; and
- Nature has its own value, regardless of its value to humanity (sacredness).

## Interactions and interdependence

- Each individual inhabits a specific area, where it interacts with other living and non-living things (**habitat**);
- Populations are organizations of interacting individuals of the same species inhabiting the same geographical area at the same time;
- Communities are interacting populations within a specified geographical region and time, forming **ecosystems;**
- A harmonious relationship between humans and environment is not only essential, for well-being, it is also intrinsic, effortless, spontaneous and natural (**interdependence**); and
- Humans are an inseparable part of the environment and we are part of the system that connects individuals, their culture and their natural surroundings.

## Environmental influences and limiting factors

- Limiting factors include radiation, climate, earth movements, and use of a homeostatic mechanism to cope with the laws of the universe like laws of thermodynamics and the forces of change in order to survive;
- **Carrying capacity** of a given resource base is the most limiting factor to population growth and increase; this capacity can be enhanced or degraded by man; and
- Changes in the environment can predictably cause responses within the levels of the organisation as they attempt to maintain homeostatic existence.

## Ecosystems and Energy flow and materials cycling in ecosystems

- Everything is connected to everything else but the resulting systems are organised into hierarchies;
- Every ecosystem has a carrying capacity beyond which the system is not sustainable;
- Carrying capacities of ecosystems can be enhanced or degraded by human activities;
- When the organisation of an ecosystem is disrupted as through exploitation, the maturity of the ecosystem declines;
- Matter /energy cannot be created or destroyed; the material of the planet stays on the planet, undergoing continuous transformations, powered by the energy of the sun and the earth. Energy flows through and matter must recycle in ecosystems;
- The materials necessary for life pass through **biogeochemical cycles** that maintain their purity and availability (natural cycles);
- Energy transformation and flow is not very efficient and there is a need for the constant influx of energy into ecosystems from the sun;
- There is a general decrease in excess potential energy and in the energy flow of biomass as ecosystems change to more mature stages; and
- The natural forces propelling the planetary cycles are enormous compared to human forces-they are easier to work with than against.

## Population dynamics

- The population as an organisational level is the basic unit of the ecosystem. Each population occupies a specific functional niche which fits into the organization of the ecosystem (e.g. as part of the energy flow and biogeochemical cycles); and
- There is a need to sustain **interspecies equity.**

## Man as a member of ecosystems

- Humans as the only living things that possess perceive and appreciate all the qualities of being-life, consciousness, self-awareness which give them special responsibility for **stewardship** of all the levels of being.
- We can measure our impact on the environment by using the **ecological footprint (EF)**. EF is a measure of the consumption of renewable natural resources by a human population. A population's EF is the total area of productive land or sea needed to produce all the crops, meat, seafood, wood and fibre it consumes, to meet its energy consumption and to give space for its infrastructure (Australian Government, 2005). The EF can be compared with the biologically productive capacity of the available land and sea to see if the population is sustainable in the long term. The measure can be applied to an individual, a family, a school, a community or the whole world. EF is an example of how we can compare the consumption of renewable resources between groups of people, be it a school, a country, or the world. For example, the average African consumer was less than 1.4 ha per person in n 1999, the average Australian was 7.i ha, and an average American was 9.6 ha. The EFP of the average world consumer in 1999 was 2.3 ha per person or 20% above the earth's biological capacity of 1.9 ha per person-i.e. humanity now exceeds the planet's capacity to sustain its consumption of renewable resources.

Key Concepts and Principles of Environmental Education for Sustainability (Environmental Conceptual Awareness)

This component focuses on the big picture of the environmental issues arising from the interaction of man with the environment. They are actually **the principles of environmental education for sustainability.** The issues are those that aim at helping the learner understand the need for social, economic, and political sustainability and their role in influencing environmental sustainability. They cut across the four sustainability categories. The major conceptual issues include the following:

*Natural Environment*: Ecosystems which include the plants and animals of an ecological community and their physical surrounds, forming an interacting system of activities and functions regarded as a unit.

*Diversity*: Variation and variety in terms of biological, cultural, social, and economic attributes and their value to the quality of human life.

*Economic Development*: This involves improvements in the efficiency of resource use so that the same or greater output of goods and services is produced with smaller throughputs of natural, manufactured and human capital.

*Interdependence*: Human beings are an inseparable part of the environment and are part of a system that connects individuals, their culture and their natural surroundings.

*Cultural Environment*: All the tangible and intangible evidence of human activity, including buildings, traditions, beliefs, religious practices, and how the cultural activities (e.g. religious, economic, political, social) influence the environment from an ecological perspective. Significant elements of the environment have cultural and historic values that may require protection from unplanned or unwise human activity.

*Ecological Sustainability*: This involves decision making processes that integrate long term and short term economic, environmental, social, and equitable considerations. It incorporates the principle of intergenerational equity—that the present generation should ensure that the health, diversity and productivity of the environment are maintained or enhanced for the benefit of future generations (Australian Government, 2005).

*Resource Management:* The natural world contains a range of resources, both renewable and non-renewable, that humans can develop and satisfy their needs and wants according to the lifestyles they adopt and with regard to the long-term sustainability of these choices.

*Values and Lifestyle Choices*: The balance of natural ecosystems and cultural heritage can be affected by unplanned or unwise human use of resources. Sometimes the problems resulting from the interactions are so severe that change in management practices and lifestyles is required to allow ecosystems to rebuild their ecological balance.

*Social Participation*: Attitudes of concern for the quality of the environment are required to motivate people to develop the skills necessary for finding out about the environment and to take the necessary actions for environmental problem-solving. This involves a deep understanding of the roles played by differing human values and the need for personal values clarification as an integral part of environmental decision making; the alternative solutions available for solving environmental issues and the ecological and cultural implications of these solutions.

*Economic Sustainability:* How economic sustainability can be achieved by adopting development that is equitable-involving the breakdown of barriers and separations between freedom and order, groups and individuals, work and play, settlement and nature. This includes a clear understanding and operation incorporating eco-efficiency, environmentally sound lifestyles, natural capital and natural resources base, accounting mechanisms, steady-state economy, sustainable consumption, and sustainable production. Overall, it involves a deep understanding of how ecological sustainability can be attained by adopting patterns of production, consumption, and reproduction that safeguards earth's regenerative capacities, human rights, and community well-being; how economic development and care of the environment are compatible, interdependent and necessary as a way of sustaining the dynamic balance between quality of life and quality of environment.

*Social Sustainability:* This includes a clear understanding and operation incorporating risk management, social justice, cultural diversity, cultural heritage, participation, intergenerational equity, peace, gender equity, human rights, and basic human needs. The ultimate goal is to galvanize every individual to adopt responsible citizenship action-e.g. persuasion, consumerism, legal action, political action and ecomanagement in the remediation of environmental issues and to be accountable for the actions in the environment.

*Political Sustainability:* The role played by the strengthened democratic space, transparency and accountability in governance, inclusive participation in social action, conflict resolution, respect for others, tolerance, proper use of power, good citizenship, peace, decision making, access to justice, and in promoting human development and social, economic, political and environmental sustainability.

*Intergenerational Equity* This is to view the human community as a partnership between all generations. It is the hallmark of sustainability in terms of meeting the needs of the present while leaving equal or better opportunities for future generations (Australian Government, 2005).

*Interspecies Equity:* Consideration of the need for humans to treat all living things decently, and to protect them from cruelty and avoidable suffering based on an understanding of humans as one of the many species on the planet Earth and that all deserve respect.:

*Quality of Life:* The standard of life that an individual enjoys. It goes beyond equating wellbeing with income. It includes such things as environmental health, the satisfaction of relationships with others and dignifying work.

*Social Justice:* This means that all people should have equal access to services and goods produced in a global community. It includes ideas of environmental health, and gender, religious, sexual, racial and ethnic equality.

*Sustainable Change:* Understanding that there is a limit to the way in which the world, particularly the richer countries, can develop, and that the consequences of unmanaged and unsustainable growth are increased poverty, and hardship and the degradation of the environment, to the disadvantage of us all(Australian Government, 2005).

*Sustainable Consumption:* The use of services and related products to satisfy basic human needs and bring a better quality of life while minimizing the use of natural resources and toxic materials as well as emissions of waste and pollutants over the life cycle of the service or product.

*Sustainable Production:* Industrial processes that transform natural resources into products that society needs in ways that minimize the resources and energy used., the waste produced and the effects of work practices and wastes on communities.

---

**Box 10.1**

---

Discussion

Understanding Social Sustainability: Conflict, Security and Peace

Do you know that social sustainability is a pillar of sustainable development? No meaningful development in the broadest sense can take place without peace and security. Peace is a condition devoid of conflicts and war. Conflict is a game played between people or communities or groups or countries and the situation is common in day to day lives of human beings.

Since conflicts are common in societies, conflict resolution is a precursor to peace. Conflicts are caused by several factors, among them deadlock over issues, aggression, hiding information, and suspicions. War and fights ensue following protracted conflicts essentially due to lack of tolerance, disagreements, and misunderstandings. Conflicts often result in an opportunity for change, learning, personal growth, community growth, new relationships and creativity. However, conflict may result in a dangerous situation such as fighting and war often with destructive consequences. It is necessary to always adopt conflict resolution and management approaches to avoid undesirable consequences of conflicts.

Conflict management approaches are divided into two broad categories: Cooperative integrative approach and competitive dichotomy or adversarial approach. In the former, the emphasis is on win/lose situation, while for the later it is a win-win situation since it is based on building trust through the provision of open information.

The cooperative approach is based on growth and creativity (win/win situation) for the parties involved in terms of dialogue (listening); needs and interests of those involved; meaningful relationships; open/direct communication; power balance is not relevant; focus on similarities and mutual aspects of the perceived differences; acceptable legitimacy; behavioural failures are; and tactics focus on care for oneself and others.

On the other hand the adversarial approach is based on a win/lose situation in terms of monologue (one-way listening); positions and claims already taken by those involved; meaningless relationships; dull, poor, and indirect communication; focus differing aspects of the perceived differences; power balance is on most relevant sources of influence; legitimacy is undetermined; behavioural failures are perceived as intended; and tactics focus on care for oneself.

Conflict resolution mechanisms occur in a continuum ranging from minimum participation of the parties to maximum participation: Court, arbitration, mediation, and negotiation. There is disengagement of the parties at court level, unilateral action at arbitration and mediation levels, and continued conflict at negotiation level. At the negotiation level, perception and beliefs of the world are influential. Other factors include: atmosphere in terms of verbal and non-verbal behaviour may also influence the atmosphere in negotiation; positions taken in terms of primary claims and demands as stated at the start of negotiation; needs and interests of the parties—the real reasons why negotiations are taking place; reframing – attempts to define the issue by focusing on the parties' interests and needs; and the contributing offers and blocking offers in the negotiations.

**Which mechanism would you prefer to employ in selected domestic and school, conflicts?**

## Environmental Investigation Skills

These are the cognitive processes that enable the learner to investigate issues and evaluate alternative solutions for resolving them. They include the following:

- Recognising and identifying environmental issues and problems using primary and secondary sources of information;
- Investigating environmental issues using various process scientific skills: observation, measurement, control of variables, modelling, data collection and recording, prediction, hypothesizing, data analysis and interpretation, inferences and communication, among

others;

- Using various instruments and equipment such as GIS and GPS, photographs and other sources of information to interpret the environment;
- Identifying alternative solutions for specific environmental problems and evaluating them in light of ecological implications; and
- Identifying, clarifying, and evaluating value positions with respect to specific environmental issues.

## Environmental Action and Participation Skills

These are skills that enable the learner to make responsible corrective decisions concerning the resolution of environmental issues. This includes preparing and evaluating action plans for resolving the issues as well as actual participation in resolving them using appropriate citizenship action strategies. The skills enable the learner to take positive environmental actions for the purpose of achieving and maintaining a dynamic balance between quality of life and quality of the environment. The skills include the following:

- Devising, implementing and evaluating action plans for environmental action;
- Making decisions regarding environmental action strategies to be used in solving specific environmental issues and problems;
- Using a variety of **environmental citizenship action skills** appropriately; and
- Evaluating the actions taken in light of their ecological implications.

## Environmental Citizenship Action Skills

### a) Negotiation

This involves an attempt to reach an agreement over an environmental issue, policy, or practice through discussion.

### b) Persuasion

Persuasion attempts to modify others viewpoints through public debate, speech making, letter writing, pamphleteering or media campaigns. Persuasion is used when an individual (or a group of people) tries to convince others that a certain environmental action is correct to undertake. Examples include:

- Convincing a friend to recycle aluminium or any other material or resource;
- Writing an environmental letter concerning a specific issue to be published in a local newspaper;
- Making and putting up posters urging people to recycle used food containers or any other material or resource; and
- Convincing parents or friends to carry their own packaging materials whenever they go shopping.

c) **Consumerism**

Consumerism is a specialised form of persuasion that relies on the power of money. It involves buying goods and services depending on whether or not, in your opinion, they impact on the environment negatively. It focuses on discriminating that social action or boycotting goods and services or economic actions aimed at changing business policy and products (Ndaruga, 2014). Examples include buying only soft drinks packaged in recyclable containers; refusing to buy products made by companies with a negative environmental record, and buying only products whose ingredients are environmentally sound.

d) **Political Action**

Political action refers to an attempt to cause political or government agencies and/or individuals, within the political framework, to take positive environmental action. This is often achieved through lobbying, voting, or supporting candidates to persuade an electorate, or legislator or government to adopt a particular environmental policy. Examples include the following:

- Writing an environmental letter to an MP urging them to support enactment of an appropriate law;
- Campaigning for a candidate with a good environmental record; and
- Voting for a pro-environment candidate.

e) **Ecomanagement**

This is the actual physical action taken to maintain or improve the quality of the environment. This could be in terms of conservation measures or environmental improvement activities undertaken. Examples are:

- Cleaning the premises of a community hospital;
- Picking and binning litter from a public park; and
- Recycling materials such as vegetable waste to form compost manure.

### f) Legal Action

This involves any legal or judicial action or legal restraint proceedings at a court of law taken by an individual or organisation aimed at some aspect of environmental enforcement or environmentally undesirable behaviour. It thus focuses on attempting to ensure the enforcement of a law or the constraining of certain behaviour by legal means. Examples include filing a court injunction against construction of a potentially dangerous factory in the community, and filing a civil suit against a factory with regard to the pollution of a given environment

The use of approaches discussed requires ethical considerations and understanding of values so that in doing so, we are careful not to be unjust or offensive to other people. Some can be taken privately, and others can be done through collaboration with members of the community. All these actions are a learning process from which to reflect on to improve later interventions (Stapp and Wals, 1993).

## Development and Organisation of Environmental Education for Sustainability Curriculum

Each school will need to plan its own curriculum appropriately. Environmental education for sustainability can be presented in the school curriculum in one or more of the following approaches: Interdisciplinary or single subject; Multi-disciplinary or infusion; and Issue-based approaches.

### Interdisciplinary Approach

By this approach, relevant components of many disciplines are drawn upon to create a distinct programme, with reference to the goals, objectives and guiding principles of environmental education for sustainability.

Advantages:

- It is easy to implement environmental education as a single subject in the curriculum;

- The approach lends itself to serious and in-depth study than when it is integrated with other subjects;
- The unity, cohesion, sequence and progression of the subject matter is ensured as learners easily see interrelationships of the components of the environment; and
- A comprehensive evaluation of environmental education is easier and more effective so as to judge the achievement of the objectives.

Disadvantages:

- The approach requires much more time on the already crowded timetable and would end up as an optional subject thus defeating its purpose;
- It would just be taken as any other subject for the purpose of passing examinations other than causing a positive impact on the environment; and
- It is difficult to get teachers capable of teaching such a highly interdisciplinary subject.

## Multidisciplinary Approach

This approach is also described as the infusion approach. In this approach, the components of environmental education for sustainability are infused into the relevant disciplines or subjects. It is the responsibility of the subject teachers to decide when the specific relevant environmental aspect should be taught within the content of their subject areas.

Advantages:

- The implementation of EE may not overload the existing curricula on the timetable; and
- Environmental concepts are taught in relation to the existing knowledge in the established subjects.

Disadvantages:

- Requires that teachers of all disciplines be competent to identify, sequence and accommodate environmental education components and adapt and use environmental education materials to achieve the goals and objectives;

- Requires greater coordination of the curriculum;
- A comprehensive evaluation of the objectives of environmental education is difficult due to the many variables involved; and
- The approach tends to deny environmental education a discipline status.

In this approach real-world situations or issues as presented in the media (print, electronic) locally, nationally or globally are selected and investigated. The issues provide a wide and varied stimulus for environmental education programmes.

An environmental issue is any subject about the environment on which there are differing opinions, beliefs, and values. It usually has social and/ or ecological significance and related in some way to the environment. Examples of environmental issues include corruption, racism, terrorism, recycling, desertification, overgrazing, over cultivation, endangered species, deforestation, female circumcision, wildlife conservation, garbage disposal, cosmetics, drug abuse, and overpopulation among others.

On the other hand, an environmental problem is usually out rightly clear and usually results from the environment itself. It manifests in the destruction of the social, built or natural environment and this destructive impact is called a natural disaster. Other problems may arise from human activity such as soil erosion, which may be caused by deforestation, overgrazing or over cultivation. In general environmental issues arise from our perceptions and the decisions we make during our interactions with the environment and give rise to environmental problems. Examples of environmental problems are floods, famine, plagues, earthquakes, soil erosion, drought, lightning, landslide, hurricanes, volcanic eruption, malaria, motor accident, HIV/AIDS.

Advantages:

- It can be used both in interdisciplinary and multidisciplinary approaches to make the curriculum more relevant and current; and
- It can be a source of stimulus for environmental action.

Disadvantages:

- Issues are multidisciplinary in orientation and may require the cooperation of several teachers in a team teaching situation; and

- Decisions have to be made by teachers regarding when and where to introduce the issues to the students. This makes many teachers to ignore the issues altogether.

## Integration

Whichever organisational approach is used, the most effective environmental education for sustainability programmes must develop learning activities outside the classroom to support and extend the classroom programme. Such activities include, but are not limited, to the following:

- Special environmental events, celebrations, and projects to complement classroom activities.
- Investigating, maintaining and improving the school and local environment.
- Using the community to investigate practical and real-life situations.
- Participating in national and international research and writing competitions on environmental issues concerning sustainability.
- Using the facilities, programmes and services of environmental education centres such as the national museum and participating in their programmes to invigorate the learning process.

## School-based Curriculum Development in Environmental Education for Sustainability

### Guiding Principles of Curriculum Planning and Development

The initiatives to promote environmental education for sustainability that should guide the rest of the planning process are as follows:

- The key concepts are clearly identified and coordinated wherever they appear in the curriculum and are reinforced through all key learning areas (**coherence**);
- Students' experiences, knowledge, attitudes and skills from their own lives and previous educational experiences are identified and inform the planning process (**prior understandings**);
- The students are enabled to relate to their surroundings as a frame of reference and are consulted about what is important and

relevant to their own lives (**relevance and connectedness**);

- The schools adopt the curriculum in response to changes and developments in the wider world (**flexibility**);
- Procedures for monitoring and evaluation are built in from the beginning (**evaluation**); and
- There is a clear progression in students' learning, matched to the needs and interests of the students and structured in developmentally appropriate ways **(progression).**

## Guiding Structural Framework of Environmental Education

A popular way of organising experiences within environmental education for sustainability programme is to adopt the environmental education structural framework: *Education about, from* and *for* the environment. This approach allows the teacher or educator to provide a range of learning opportunities for dialogue, encounters, and reflection using a variety of techniques.

### Education about the environment

This refers to the learning process that seeks to promote the acquisition of information concerning the environment. Its functions include helping students to:

- Acquire knowledge and understanding of how natural systems work: the key facts, concepts and theories;
- Understand the impact of human activities upon these systems; and
- Develop environmental awareness and concerns.

Example:

In handling the topic 'Tea farming in Kericho' from this perspective the teacher is only interested in finding out how tea is cultivated, the conditions necessary for its cultivation, how it is processed and exported. The teacher does not need to take the students to the area to get this information.

### Education from the environment

This refers to the use of the environment as a teaching resource to provide relevant learning experiences. In this way, the learner is expected to gain a great deal of knowledge and understanding as well as skills of investigation and communication.

Example:

Concerning tea farming, in Kericho, the teacher will be expected to take students to Kericho to see the actual tea farming activities. The students are expected to ask questions about the activities and to collect relevant information often guided by a pre-prepared questionnaire. The function of this perspective is to help students to:

- Give reality, relevance and practical experience to learning through direct contact with the environment;
- Develop important skills in data collection and field investigations.
- Develop aesthetic appreciation.

**Education for the Environment**

This refers to learning that involves the identification of actual problems in the environment and seeking solutions to them and attempting to solve them. The purpose is to educate the learners so that their actions and influences on collective action will be positive for the benefit of the environment. This perspective helps the students to:

- Develop an informal concern and sense of responsibility for the environment;
- Develop the motivation and skills to participate in environmental improvement;
- Develop values which affect behaviour leading formation of a personal environmental ethic; and
- Be compatible with the wise use of environmental resources.

Example:

From this perspective, the lesson on tea farming in Kericho will involve encouraging students to go beyond the acquisition of knowledge and skills of investigation. Apart from getting information about tea farming through questioning students also identify the environmental effects of tea cultivation and processing and the possible ways of solving the problems. The following observations can be made:

- Education about and from the environment facilitates the learner's acquisition of knowledge and investigation skills about the environment, but they do not help them to cultivate skills in decision making and action in the environment. They are knowledge-based, i.e. learning concepts without creating a concern for the environment;

- It is only when education for the environment is actually taking place that the essence of environment education is achieved; and

- Environmental education is a process of learning about, from and for the environment.

## Steps in School-based Curriculum Development in Environmental Education for Sustainability

In Kenya, the multidisciplinary approach is usually used to incorporate environmental issues in the regular school curriculum. However, an analysis of the distribution of environmental issues in the school subjects indicates that some subjects such as mathematics, religious studies, business studies, computer studies, history and government, chemistry and physics have a very small proportion of the issues. In such cases, teachers may wish to incorporate issues that are not included in their subjects. Even for those subjects like geography and biology that have a good proportion of the components of environmental education, the teachers may still wish to incorporate some current issues which keep coming up. Whatever the situation, teachers must prepare their schemes of work and lesson plans diligently in order to achieve the goals and objectives of environmental education for sustainability through their subject areas. The two key steps in the process of planning what to teach are Content Analysis and Concept Webbing.

### Content Analysis

Content Analysis refers to the assessment of a given topic in the subject area and the relevant curriculum materials to determine the concepts and ideas involved. If an environmental topic is already laid out in the curriculum materials then the content analysis need not be done. However, where the materials don't indicate environmental topics to be taught the teacher will need to select the issue, which is usually a current environmental issue of concern, and carry out an elaborate content analysis to determine the concepts and ideas that can be taught through one or more of the topics in the subject area. The key environmental concepts and ideas are then identified and displayed by constructing a concept web.

## Concept Web

The environmental concepts, subconcepts and ideas are developed by relating them to the existing concepts and ideas in the subject area. These are appropriately linked by joining them using lines.

If we take **drug abuse** as an issue the various teachers wish to incorporate in their subjects, then the resulting distribution of the concepts and ideas that can be identified will be as summarised Table 10.2.

**Table 10.2: Concepts and Ideas Constructed on the theme of Drug and Drug Abuse**

| Subject | Topic | Subtopic | Environmental Concept |
|---|---|---|---|
| Mathematics | Measurement | Measuring, computation and graphing | The lifespan of drug abusers; Rates of increase of cases of drug abuse; Frequency of cases; Means and standard deviations of cases; Proportion of cases affected by age, gender, etc; Proportions of deaths by gender, age. |
| Biology | Human Health and Diseases | Psychosomatic and nervous diseases | Social degradation and social sustainability: Drug addiction, Effects of drugs, Control of drug abuse. |
| Physical sciences | Chemical analyses and instrumentation | Chemical composition and effects of substances | Effects of various types of drugs |
| Languages | Drama | The plot, plays, acting | Dramatising causes and effects of drug abuse; |
| | Poetry | Constructing | Dramatising control of drug |

| | Grammar | poems | abuse; |
|---|---|---|---|
| | | Communication skills Comprehension | Poems on the causes and effects of drug abuse; Composition on causes and effects of drug abuse; Passages on drug abuse |
| Geography | Human geography: Population dynamics | Population barriers to development: Graphing; Mapping; and Distribution | Social sustainability: cases of drug abuse by % by age and gender; Distribution of cases using maps, figures. |
| Business studies | Factors of production | Labour supply and productivity | Social and economic sustainability: the need for a healthy and productive society |
| History and government | Control of crimes | Social factors in crime: historical developments | Social sustainability: Advances in control of drug usage |
| Creative Arts | Presentation of information | Songs, Printing and Collage | Social sustainability: warning songs against drug abuse; songs depicting agony experienced by drug abusers; posters showing victims of drug abuse; messages in college on drug abuse. |
| Home science | Nutrition | Nutrition for various categories of | Social sustainability: Rehabilitation |

| | | people | programmes for victims of drug abuse |
|---|---|---|---|

## Summary

This chapter has shown that environmental education for sustainability curriculum involves understanding the present environment (how it has been shaped, the value in which it's held, and seeking to mitigate adverse effects on it). This involves an exploration of the local environment to understand how we have come to this state and accepting responsibility to work towards a sustainable future. This approach helps to understand the local community's environmental issues and the role of the school in mitigating the issues. With this background information, the curriculum is then modelled to increase students' engagement through relevant practical activities mainly outside the classroom while taking account of their lives and interests.

The chapter outlines how environmental education for sustainability can be developed, organised and implemented in such a manner that learners are provided practical learning opportunities to fully participate in sustainable development. You will be able to understand how environmental education is incorporated into the school curriculum and the approaches used in teaching environmental education from a sustainability perspective.

## End of Chapter Activities

For a concept such as HIV/AIDS, construct a concept web to help you decide what you can teach through your subject area in terms of environmental education for sustainability.

## Bibliography

Arms, K. (1994)
     *Environmental Science*, 2nd Edn.  Fort Worth: Saunders College Publishing.
Australian Government (2005)
     Educating for a Sustainable Future: A National Environmental Education Statement for Australian Schools. Carlton South: Commonwealth of Australia
Australian Government (2007)

Caring for Our Future: The Australian Government Strategy for the United Nations Decade of Education for Sustainable Development, 2005-2014. Canberra: Commonwealth of Australia

Commonwealth of Australia (2000)
Environmental Education for a Sustainable Future: A National Action Plan. Canberra: Environment Education Unit

Cunningham, W. P. and Saigo, B.W. (2001)
Environmental Science: _A Global Concern_. Boston: McGraw Hill (6th Edn)

Korir- Koech, M (1988):
Environmental Education PAC 101 Faculty of External Degree Studies, University of Nairobi.

McKinney, M.L. and Schoch, R. M. (1998)
_Environmental Science: Systems and Solutions,_ Boston: Jones and Bartlett (web-enhanced Edn).

Muyanda-Mutebi, P(Ed)
Environmental Education: A Teaching and Training Guide Pan Africa Books.

Muthoka, M, Rego and Rimbui, Z (1998)
Environmental Education: Essential knowledge for Sustainable Development. Longhorn

Odum, E.P. (1971)
Fundamentals of Ecology. W.A Sanders.

Otiende, J.E. et al. (1991)
Environmental Education Nairobi University Press

Turk, J. & Turk, A (1984)
_Environmental Science_, 3rd Edn. Philadelphia: Saunders College Publishing.

UNESCO (1980)
Environmental Education in the Light of Tbilisi Conference.

# 11

## CHAPTER 11

# INSTRUCTION IN ENVIRONMENTAL EDUCATION FOR SUSTAINABILITY

### Introduction

This chapter outlines how environmental education for sustainability can be implemented. It is not uncommon to teach in such a manner that learners are provided with practical learning opportunities to fully participate in sustainable development. You will be able to understand how to teach the often abstract concepts through concrete case studies of local, national or global examples in order to make them more meaningful in relation to the students' everyday lives and practical experiences. You will learn that a whole-school approach is the most favoured, working across all curriculum areas and activities.

## Effective Teaching and Learning for Sustainability

Environmental education for sustainability aims at empowering students to create a sustainable future. This is possible if the students' are exposed to active and self-directed learning situations that enhance their knowledge, skills, values, actions and ethically responsible citizenship (Australian Government, 2005). Environmental education for sustainability generates action by challenging pupils, on a personal level, to change parts of their lives so that they are engaged in leading more sustainable lifestyles (Ndaruga, 2014). At a public level, they are encouraged to take responsibility for the care and management of the environment directly through participation in practical conservation projects or indirectly as informed and concerned adults through the democratic process (Tilbury, 1995). The instructional approaches that promote such situations will help the students to become: reflective, creative and deep thinkers; autonomous but connected learners; and ethical and responsible citizens in their actions.

According to the Australian Government (2005), a *reflective* and *deep thinker* is a student that makes sense of and understands the complexity and holistic nature of environmental concepts and the interdependence of ideas underpinning sustainability. On the other hand, an *autonomous learner* is self-directed and motivated, with an ongoing interest in learning more about the environment, while a *connected learner* is engaged, interested and enthusiastic about exploring the world around them and capable of working cooperatively with others. A student is *an ethical and responsible* citizen when he or she is empathetic to others and is able to make ethical decisions about environmental issues, events and actions (Australian Government, 2005), (see Figure 11.1).

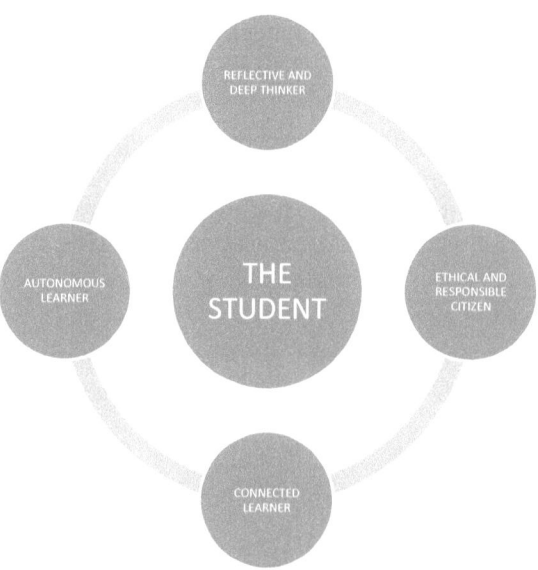

Figure 11.1: The Four Products of Active Learning in Environmental Education for Sustainability (Adapted from Australian Government, 2005)

It requires effective teachers to achieve the four dimensions of the learner as outlined above. Such teachers must have special qualities and are those who will:

- Encourage higher order and critical thinking about environmental knowledge;
- Promote deep understanding of environmental knowledge;
- Talks confidently about such knowledge and how it relates to attitudes, values, action and participation;
- Encourages students to communicate environmental ideas clearly and confidently;
- Considers social justice, diversity, and equitability issues when reflecting on classroom and school practices;
- Strives to model desirable behaviour towards the environment;
- Encourages students to actively participate in school and community environmental management;
- Helps students to develop a positive vision for themselves and their future;
- Provides opportunities for students to connect to the local and global environment;
- Builds on students' experiences, awareness and prior

understandings of the environment;

- Integrates knowledge about the ecological, social, political and economic systems;
- Helps students to formulate constructive futures for themselves and others;
- Provides opportunities for students to consider the impact of scientific and technological innovations and their applications;
- Guides students to learn rather than instructing them;
- Encourages student autonomy and self-direction;
- Provides a supportive, democratic learning environment; and
- Participates with students in the learning process.

It is now necessary to describe some of the instructional approaches teachers may use to realise all these best practice features.

## Instructional Methods, Techniques and Strategies used

The terms 'methods', 'technique' and 'strategy' are often loosely used by teachers to "ways of teaching". However, these terms refer to different though related activities.

### Teaching Method

A teaching method refers to a general approach to conducting a lesson. There are two general methods of teaching: Expository and Problem-solving. Expository (or transmission) method is where the teacher largely provides the information. Problem-solving method is where the students search for answers and information.

### Teaching Technique

A teaching technique refers to the specific actions and processes through which the teaching method is realised.

Examples:

| **Method** | | **Technique** |
|---|---|---|
| (a) | Expository | Lecture, Recitation, Discussion, Demonstration |
| (b) | Problem-Solving | Grouping, Debate, Panel discussion, Experiments |

## Teaching Strategy

This refers to the sequencing or ordering of the techniques a teacher has selected to teach a lesson. Variety in teaching techniques increases the chances of reaching more students. For example, in a lesson, a teacher may order techniques as followings:

- Introductory lecture;
- Grouping;
- Panel discussion; and
- Summary lecture.

Students cannot change their behaviour and become effective and responsible citizens when only lecture and discussion techniques are used in the teaching and learning process. For example, learners cannot be expected to investigate issues unless they have the skills needed for, and experience in, the process of issue investigation. Similarly, they cannot be skilled and responsible decision makers unless they are acquainted with a decision – making processes and are provided with opportunities to apply those skills. The challenge is, therefore, to provide a wide range of effective learning experiences, using a wide range of teaching techniques, which promote and support environmental education for sustainability.

Some teaching techniques in environmental education are more appropriate than others in giving the desired outcomes. Such techniques are student centred and are highly interactive within and beyond the classroom. If correctly used these techniques help to develop in the students: A sense of environmental care; willingness to act positively in the environment; and a commitment to life-sustaining rather than life-destroying thought and action.

The most commonly used techniques that are supportive of environmental education for sustainability include, but are not limited, to the following:

- Field course excursions;
- Affective techniques: Values clarification (issue analysis); Moral dilemma; Jurisprudence;
- Simulation games (including role play);
- Issue-based instruction (case study);
- Panel discussions;
- Debates; and

175

- Action projects.

## Affective Techniques

*Values Clarification and Analysis*

This approach is used to deal with controversial environmental issues in a balanced and sensitive manner. It is an approach that encourages students to analyse their own thoughts and opinions about an environmental issue, while values analysis encourages students to think about and analyse a range of perspectives in relation to their own. This is the process one goes through as one inspects the bases for a value perspective (Australian Government, 2005).

In this technique, the teacher explores the student's positions with regard to environmental issues or problems. This is usually done through a series of questions and probes during the learning process. As the students get new information they change their values where necessary. Students can be encouraged and supported to explore such controversial issues as spirituality, the sacredness of place and the stewardship of finite resources. Group work and individual attention are essential in this approach.

Other techniques such as role – play, games and simulations of real-life situations, in-depth self-analysis exercises, out – of class activities and small group discussion can be used in values clarification. Important steps in values clarification include:

- Choosing an appropriate issue;
- Reviewing literature on the issue;
- Identifying the values issues that are best illustrated by the issue;
- Selecting an appropriate activity format;
- Reducing the activity to clear directions for students and brief introductory statements of content;
- Fitting the activity to the time available; and
- Following activity with a discussion.

Let us take tree planting in homes as one of the controversial issues in our cultures. It is generally held that females should plant and own trees in our homesteads. However, we know that trees are an essential part of the environment as they form a link in the food chain and in the carbon cycle. In the analysis, we are expected to understand our values in this respect and the consensus we should arrive at. This is achieved through questioning ourselves along these lines: Why are trees planted in their homes? Have you planted trees in your homes? If yes, why? If not, why not? How can you help them change their views/beliefs? Values clarification can help learners to:

- Become aware of and identify their own values and those of others;
- Communicate openly and honestly with others about their values; and
- Use both rational thinking and emotional awareness to examine their personal feelings, values and behaviour patterns.

## Moral Dilemma

More often than not environmental management directly touches on our moral values. Students are undergoing moral development and should be aided in this process through environmental education for sustainability by being exposed to moral conflict situations (moral dilemma).

Take an example of the conflict that arises between communities and wildlife in Kenya. Monkeys are some of the wild animals that precipitate such conflict. For the students to be helped to understand the situation, tasks that enable them to see the right of survival for the monkeys should be provided to the students. If monkeys destroy crops should they be killed? What is the consensus? Knowledge of biodiversity conservation should be the basis of any arguments in this activity.

## Jurisprudence

This technique employs legal procedures and arguments in resolving environmental issues. The students should have knowledge of the laws of Kenya, particularly environmental laws, the bill of rights, freedoms of persons and legal procedures. The students should plan for this kind of activity thoroughly.

Consider the example of a person who takes the law in his own hands by brutally injuring another person who has just cut a tree in the former's farm. The students are helped to understand this situation through a series of questions such as: Are we justified to flog a person who has cut our tree without permission? Are there other alternative measures? Are we justified to accuse a person who cuts down a tree in a court of law? What are the legal provisions for this offence? What is the consensus about these issues?

## Simulation and Role Play

Simulation is a game although there are no winners or losers. It is an imitation of a situation. Role play is often a part of the simulation, whereby people act roles in a simulated situation. The teacher is expected to design a simulated situation that gives an opportunity to the students to discuss the issue and arrive at a consensus. Positions or roles have to be taken up by selected students who then look up the relevant information for presentation. For better results, the students selected in the various roles should prepare thoroughly.

Example:

Imagine that it has been noted with great concern that a number of middle-aged women dying of kidney failure are on the increase. Scientists and doctors think that this is due to the use of Beauty Cosmetics products. The Ministry of Health is contemplating to ban the use of this product. You wish to make your position clear to the Ministry. A meeting of experts has been arranged whereby a consensus on the issue is to be reached and a recommendation taken to the Ministry. Prepare your defence.

Positions Represented:

- Ministry of Health;
- Medical Practitioner;
- Maendeleo ya Wanawake leader;
- Beauty Cosmetics Manager;
- Pharmacologist;
- Ministry of Industry;
- Environmentalist;
- School girls' representative; and
- School boys' representative.

## Panel Discussions

A panel consists of a number of students assigned to act as a team to research and present their findings on a particular environmental issue. The panel orally reports the findings on the issue to the class. The panel differs from the debate in that it is not intended as a means of stimulating debate among the panel members, but rather, as a systematic way for a team of students to research and present their report on an issue. For example, a group of students may be tasked to investigate and report to the class the incidences of waterborne diseases in the local area. The students carry out activities such as finding out reasons for the spread of diseases and visiting dispensaries, hospitals and clinics to collect data on the issue.

## Debate

This is when students apply their knowledge and attitudes to give opposing views on an environmental issue. In order to defend their positions, students should pre-plan thoroughly to make it as competitive and as real as possible. For example, they may be asked to prepare arguments on the topic: "The application of chemical fertilisers in crop production is better than the application of manure". The debate should be as competitive as possible by splitting the class into two opposing groups.

## Action Projects

To be more effective projects should relate to community environmental problems. It should also involve community members as resource persons and as active participants. The project can be undertaken by one or several groups of students. The projects may include landscaping of school compound; planting trees in school and community; planting flowers; erecting and labelling signposts in school compound; constructing a pond in school or community; cleaning up a market place or hospital premises; and making litter bins and positioning them in school compound among others.

## Problem Based Learning

Inquiry learning based on a specific problem or issue encourages learners to respond to their own concern or curiosity and to investigate and act on an environmental issue. The issue should be real and based in the community or school environment. The teacher is expected to carefully develop the inquiry tasks, including the use of simulations, pictures, photographs, clippings from newspapers and magazines. Students are encouraged to think through and solve problems associated with that issue. They are responsible for collecting and analysing data in order to reach their own conclusions and to decide on appropriate courses of environmental action (social action).

Box 11.1

Discussion

## Understanding Social Sustainability

Do you know that we are unable to cause a change in our lifestyles and adopt sustainability in our lives because of our inner selves? What is the cause of all this?

The factors are both internal and external to each one of us:

**Internal factors:**

Motivation/drive
Self-confidence
Creativity
Initiative
Language mastery
Critical thought
Faith
Mental capacity
Belief
Connectivity
Self-judgment

**External factors**

Employer
Money
Opportunities
Destiny
 Education/learning
Exposure
Family
Culture
Bureaucracy
 Media/advertisements

Present the internal factors diagrammatically in a hierarchical manner. Explain how you would overcome the inner factors so that a change in your behaviour is made possible. What of external factors, what would you do to overcome their influence over your behaviour?

## Lesson planning in Environmental Education for Sustainability

The following steps should be taken in the process of lesson planning.

- Preparing instructional objectives in terms of knowledge, skills and attitudes. The knowledge objectives focus on education about the environment, while skills objectives focus on education from and for the environment. Attitudinal objectives mainly address experiences on education for the environment;

- Developing learning tasks and experiences that focus on education *about, from* and *for* the environment;
- Selecting the teaching techniques and strategies to be used to achieve the desired outcomes; and
- Compiling or writing up the lesson plan.

## Instructional Objectives

The instructional objectives should establish what the student is to learn. They should specify the knowledge to be covered, and the skills and attitudes to be developed. For example, in the case of a lesson in biology on drug abuse, the following objectives would be developed:

**Knowledge objectives**:

By the end of the lesson, students should be able to:

- Define the terms 'drug' and 'drug abuse';
- Classify drugs according to their effects on the human body; and
- State all the five major effects of drugs on the human nervous system.

**Skill objectives:**

By the end of the lesson students should be able to:

- Plan a survey on the prevalence of drug abuse in the community surrounding the school;
- Collect, analyse and interpret data on the use of drugs in the community;
- Write a report of the survey on drug use and abuse in the community; and
- Make campaign posters against drug abuse for use in the community.

**Attitudinal objectives:**

By the end of the lesson students should be able to:

- Appreciate the problem of drug abuse in the community;

- Improve community awareness about drug abuse;
- Make a campaign against drug abuse in the community; and
- Counsel drug abuse victims in the community.

## Developing Learning Tasks and Experiences

These are the students' learning activities that will help the teacher to achieve the objectives. These tasks and experiences should educate the learner *about, from* and *for* the environment. Within this framework, the activities will help the learner to gain personal experience in the environment (education about and from the environment), show personal concern for the environment (education about and for the environment) and take action in and on behalf of the environment (education from and for the environment). The learning experiences are of three categories:

- *Direct experiences*: students are involved in hands-on activities in the environment. These include action research in the community using interviews and observations;
- *Indirect experiences*: the students are encouraged to find out from secondary sources and listening to guest speakers and resource persons; and
- *Action and participation experiences:* the students participate in fostering environmental protection and improvement. These may be classroom activities or action projects. Classroom activities may include debates, writing letters, making posters, role plays, simulations, games regarding various environmental issues. Action projects in the school or community environment will be those related to the issues taught to allow students to apply what they have learned in improving the quality of the environment.

For a biology lesson on drug and drug abuse, some of the learning tasks and experiences would include the following base on the framework of education about, from and for the environment (Table 11.1).

Table 11.1: Preparation of Lesson Plan on Drug and Drug Abuse

| ORGANISATIONAL APPROACH | LESSON CONTENT | LEARNING TASKS/EXPERIENCES |
|---|---|---|
| Education about the environment | -Definition of drug and drug abuse -Types of drugs | -Whole class or group discussions -Viewing pictures, films, posters Reading about drugs and |

| | -Effects of drugs on the nervous system<br>-Factors promoting drug abuse<br>-Effects of long-term use of drugs | drug abuse<br>-Making notes<br>-Raising questions about drugs |
|---|---|---|
| Education from the environment | -Determining the magnitude of drug abuse in the community<br>-Determining attitudes of students and community towards drug abuse | -Observations to appreciate drug abuse problem<br>-Developing a questionnaire to collect data<br>-planning a survey<br>-Carrying out the survey through interviews, observations<br>-Recording data<br>-Writing a report |
| Education for the environment | -Promoting the anti-drug abuse campaign<br>-Prevention of spread of drug abuse<br>-Rehabilitation of drug abuse victims<br>-Improving community awareness of drug use and abuse | -Making campaign posters about drug abuse<br>-Carrying out a campaign against drug abuse<br>-Counselling drug abuse victims |

# Factors Affecting Successful Implementation of Environmental Education for Sustainability in Secondary Schools in Kenya

## Teaching Methods

The teaching approach used to teach about environmental issues in our secondary schools is mainly deductive. The teacher primarily conveys information with students being passive recipients. This approach fosters the acquisition of environmental knowledge but disregards the development of environmental action skills on one hand and concern for the environment on the other. Teachers thus emphasise education ABOUT the environment rather than education FOR the environment.

## Constraints of teaching about Environmental issues

- Many teachers are not well trained to handle environmental issues in the classroom;
- Examinations do not emphasise practical aspects of environmental action. This discourages students' participation in environmental action;
- Cultural values tend to inhibit participation by some students in environmental action. For example, girls are not allowed to plant trees or repair houses. This discourages students' application of knowledge and skills in solving environmental problems;
- A majority of the schools do not have environmental education programs. Hence there is no co-ordination regarding the teaching and learning of environmental issues in the various subject areas and the co-curricular activities performed by students through clubs;
- Curriculum congestion tends to inhibit students' participation in practical activities in the environment. There is no extra time set aside for such activities; and
- Some teachers and students may simply not be interested in environmental activities (apathy).

## A Paradigm Shift in Teacher Training

For teachers to effectively participate in ensuring that environmental education for sustainability is achieved the teacher trainees will need to change from the traditional practice of "Learning about to learning with and learning from." This is achieved by ensuring:

- Inner motivation/drive to make a change is encouraged (moving from activism to motivation)
- People and students work together for social change.
- Creation of a process and a framework where students/people learn and work together i.e. process oriented toward social change through joint social entrepreneurship.

The stages involved in this enterprise include the following:

- Knowing one another through the process of mutual acquaintance and creative activity and dialogue. This creates a deep understanding of the students and the teacher;
- Learning from success stories from others from the community and other parts of the world as reported in the media and digital platforms (e.g. TED, YouTube, etc.);
- Designing the enterprise by developing new initiatives; planning projects and developing projects-i.e. transforming a dream and ideas into written plan and project that will come into being in the future; and
- Transformation whereby life changes in terms of the personal attributes, professional acumen, the school, and the training institution. The personal attributes include knowing own limits, independence and self-acceptance. The professional attributes include professional development, doing things differently, and knowing that you don't know. The trainee also develops personal leadership skills as an educator.

## Summary

This chapter has outlined how environmental education for sustainability is taught across the curriculum. Since environmental education for sustainability aims at empowering students to create a sustainable future the students' are exposed to active and self-directed learning situations that enhance their knowledge, skills, values, actions and ethically responsible citizenship. The instructional approaches that promote such situations will help the students to become: reflective, creative and deep thinkers; autonomous but connected learners; and ethical and responsible citizens in their actions. It's not uncommon to teach in such a manner that learners are provided practical learning opportunities to fully participate in sustainable development. You have seen that you will be required to teach the often abstract concepts through concrete case studies of local, national or global examples in order to make them more meaningful in relation to the students' everyday lives and practical experiences.

## End of Chapter Activities

- Explore, giving examples, the interactive instructional techniques you would use to teach various selected environmental education for sustainability concepts; and
- Explain the changes we need to make in environmental education in order to make environmental education for sustainability successful.

## BIBLIOGRAPHY

Australian Government (2005)
    Educating for a Sustainable Future: A National Environmental
    Education Statement for Australian Schools. Carlton South:
    Commonwealth of Australia
Australian Government (2007)
    Caring for Our Future: The Australian Government Strategy for
    the United Nations Decade of Education for Sustainable
    Development, 2005-2014. Canberra: Commonwealth of Australia
Commonwealth of Australia (2000)
    Environmental Education for a Sustainable Future: A National
    Action Plan. Canberra: Environment Education Unit.
Korir- Koech, M (1988)
    Environmental Education PAC 101 Faculty of External Degree
    Studies, University of Nairobi.
Muyanda-Mutebi, P(Ed)
    Environmental Education: A Teaching and Training Guide Pan
    Africa Books.
Muthoka, M, Rego and Rimbui, Z (1998)
    Environmental Education: Essential Knowledge for Sustainable
    Development. Longhorn
Otiende, J.E. et al. (1991)
    Environmental Education Nairobi University Press
UNESCO (1980)
    Environmental Education in the Light of Tbilisi Conference.

# 12

## CHAPTER 12

## SUSTAINABILITY: RECONCILING THE EARTH CHARTER AND SUSTAINABLE DEVELOPMENT GOALS

### Introduction

The development model that has hitherto encouraged wasteful patterns of production and consumption are causing unprecedented environmental destruction, depletion of resources and extinction of species. In addition, vices such as a steep rise in population, inequitable distribution of resources, injustice, poverty, ignorance, and violent conflict are widespread and the cause of ecological, social, economic and political instability. The fabric of global security is threatened. The need for the creation of sustainable communities is now more compelling than ever before. In order to build a sustainable global community, the nations of the world must fully abide by the international agreements and support the implementation of major guidelines and principles for sustainable living such as those espoused in the Earth Charter and Sustainable Development Goals (SDGs). This chapter provides a critical analysis of the fundamental principles and goals for sustainable living contained in the Earth Charter and SDGs.

## The Earth Charter

### Mission

The mission of The Earth Charter is to "establish a sound ethical foundation for the emerging global society and to help build a sustainable world based on respect for nature, diversity, universal human rights, economic justice and culture of peace". It is essentially a declaration of fundamental principles for building a just, sustainable and peaceful global society in the 21st century.

### Rationale

The dominant patterns of production and consumption are causing environmental devastation, the depletion of resources and a massive extinction of species. Communities are being undermined. The benefits of development are not shared equitably and the gap between rich and poor is widening. Injustice, poverty, ignorance, and violent conflict are widespread and the cause of great suffering. An unprecedented rise in human population has overburdened ecological and social systems. The foundations of global security are threatened. These trends are perilous but not inevitable.

    The Earth is becoming increasingly interdependent and fragile and the future, therefore, holds great peril as well as great promise. Humanity is part of a vast evolving universe. Earth our home is alive with a unique community of life. The forces of nature make existence a demanding and uncertain adventure, but Earth has provided the conditions essential to life's evolution. The resilience of the community of life and the wellbeing of humanity depend upon preserving a healthy biosphere with all its ecological systems, a rich variety of plants and animals, fertile soils, pure waters and clean air. The global environment with its finite resources is a common concern of all peoples. The protection of Earth's vitality, diversity and beauty is a sacred trust.

    To move forward we must recognise that in the midst of a magnificent diversity of cultures and life forms we are one human family and one Earth community with a common destiny. We must join together to bring forth a sustainable global society founded on respect for nature, universal rights, economic justice and culture of peace. Towards the end, it is imperative that we the peoples of Earth declare our responsibility to one another to the greater community of life and to future generations.

## The Challenges Ahead

The choice is ours: form a global partnership to care for Earth and one another or risk the destruction of ourselves and the diversity of life. Fundamental changes are needed in our values, institutions, and ways of living. We must realise that when basic needs have been met, human development is primarily about being more, not having more. We have the knowledge and technology to provide for all and to reduce our impacts on the environment. The emergence of global civil society is creating new opportunities to build a democratic and humane world. Our environmental, economic, political, social and spiritual challenges are interconnected and together we can forge inclusive solutions.

## Universal Responsibility

To realise these aspirations, we must decide to live with a sense of universal responsibility, identifying ourselves with the whole Earth community as well as our local communities. We are at once citizens of different nations and of one world in which the local and global are linked. Everyone shares responsibility for the present and future well-being of the human family and the larger living world. The spirit of human solidarity and kinship with all life is strengthened when we live with reverence for the mystery of being, gratitude for the gift of life, and humanity regarding the human place of nature.

We urgently need a shared vision of basic values to provide an ethical foundation for the emerging world community. Therefore, together in hope, we affirm the following interdependent principles for a sustainable way of life as a common standard by which the conduct of all individuals, organisations, businesses, governments, and transnational institutions is to be guided and assessed.

## The Way Forward

As never before in history common destiny beckons us to seek a new beginning. Such renewal is the promise of these Earth Charter principles. To fulfil this promise, we must commit ourselves to adopt and promote the values and objectives of the Charter.

This requires a change of mind and heart. It requires a new sense of global interdependence and universal responsibility. We must imaginatively develop and apply the vision of a sustainable way of life locally, nationally, regionally and globally. Our cultural diversity is a precious heritage and different cultures will find their own distinctive ways to realize the vision. We must deepen and expand the global dialogue that generated the Earth Charter, for we have much to learn from the ongoing collaborative search for truth and wisdom.

Life often involves tensions between important values. This can mean difficult choices. However, we must find ways to harmonise diversity with unity, the exercise of freedom with the common good, short-term objectives with long-term goals. Every individual, family, organization and community has a vital role to play. The arts, sciences, religions, educational institutions, media, businesses, nongovernmental organizations, and governments are all called to offer creative leadership. The partnership of government, civil society and business are essential for effective governance.

In order to build a sustainable global community, the nations of the world must renew their commitment to the United Nations, fulfil their obligations under existing international agreements, and support the implementation of Earth Charter principles with an international legally binding instrument on environment and development.

Let ours be the time remembered for the awakening of a new reverence for life, the firm resolve to achieve sustainability, the quickening of the struggle for justice and peace, and the joyful celebration of life.

## PRINCIPLES

### I.     RESPECT AND CARE FOR THE COMMUNITY OF LIFE

#### 1)   Respect Earth and life in all its diversity

a)  Recognise that all beings are interdependent and every form of life has value regardless of its worth to human beings; and

b)  Affirm faith in the inherent dignity of all human beings and in the intellectual, artistic, ethical and spiritual potential of humanity.

#### 2) Care for the community of life with understanding, compassion and love

a)  Accept that with the right to own, manage and use natural resources comes the duty to prevent environmental harm and to protect the rights of people; and

b)  Affirm that with increased freedom, knowledge and power comes increased responsibility to promote the common good.

### 3) Build democratic societies that are just, participatory, sustainable and peaceful

a) Ensure that communities at all levels guarantee human rights and fundamental freedoms and provide everyone with an opportunity to realise his or her full potential; and
b) Promote social and economic justice, enabling all to achieve a secure and meaningful livelihood that is ecologically responsible.

### 4) Secure Earth's bounty and beauty for present and future generations

a) Recognise that the freedom of action of each generation is qualified by the needs of future generations; and
b) Transmit to future generations values, traditions and institutions that support the long term flourishing of Earth's human and ecological communities.

In order to fulfil these four broad commitments, it is necessary to:

## II.    ECOLOGICAL INTEGRITY

### 5) Protect and restore the integrity of Earth's ecological systems, with special concern for biological diversity and the natural process that sustain life.

a) Adopt at all levels sustainable development plans and regulations that make environmental conservation and rehabilitation integral to all development initiatives;
b) Establish and safeguard viable nature and biosphere reserves, including wild lands and marine areas, to protect Earth's life support systems, maintain diversity, and preserve our natural heritage;
c) Promote the recovery of endangered species and ecosystems;
d) Control and eradicate non-native or genetically modified organisms harmful to native species and the environment and prevent the introduction of such harmful organisms;
e) Manage the use of renewable resources such as water, soil, forest products and marine life in ways that do not exceed rates of regeneration and that protect the health of ecosystems; and
f) Manage the extraction and use of non-renewable resources such as

mineral and fossil fuels in ways that minimise depletion and cause no serious environmental damage.

**6) Prevent harm as the best method of environmental protection and, when knowledge is limited, apply a precautionary approach.**

a) Take action to avoid the possibility of serious or irreversible environmental harm even when scientific knowledge is incomplete or inconclusive;
b) Place the burden of proof on those who argue that a proposed activity will not cause significant harm and make the responsible parties liable for environmental harm;
c) Ensure that decision making addresses the cumulative, long-term, indirect, long distance and global consequences of human activities;
d) Prevent pollution of any part of the environment and allow no build-up of radioactive, toxic or other hazardous substances; and
e) Avoid military activities damaging to the environment.

**7) Adopt patterns of production, consumption and reproduction that safeguard Earth's regenerative capacities, human rights and community well-being.**

a) Reduce, reuse and recycle the materials used in production and consumption systems and ensure that residual waste can be assimilated by ecological systems;
b) Act with restraint and efficiency when using energy, and rely increasingly on renewable energy sources such as solar and wind;
c) Promote the development, adoption and equitable transfer of environmentally sound technologies;
d) Internalise the full environmental and social costs of goods and services in the selling price and enable consumers to identify products that meet the highest social and environmental standards;
e) Ensure universal access to health care that fosters reproductive health and responsible reproduction; and
f) Adopt lifestyles that emphasise the quality of life and material sufficiency in a finite world.

**8) Advance the study of ecological sustainability and promote the open exchange and wide application of the**

**knowledge acquired.**

a) Support international scientific and technical cooperation on sustainability with special attention to the needs of developing nations;

b) Recognise and preserve the traditional knowledge and spiritual wisdom in all cultures that contribute to environmental protection and human wellbeing; and

c) Ensure that information of vital importance to human health and environmental protection including genetic information remains available in the public domain.

## III.    SOCIAL AND ECONOMIC JUSTICE

### 9) Eradicate poverty as an ethical, social and environmental imperative.

a) Guarantee the right to potable water, clean air, food security, uncontaminated soil, shelter, and safe sanitation, allocating the national and international resources required;

b) Empower every human being with the education and resources to secure a sustainable livelihood and provide social security and safety nets for those who are unable to support themselves; and

c) Recognise the ignored, protect the vulnerable, serve those who suffer and enable them to develop their capacities and to pursue their aspirations.

### 10) Ensure that economic activities and institutions at all levels promote human development in an equitable and sustainable manner.

a) Promote the equitable distribution of wealth within nations and among nations;

b) Enhance the intellectual, financial, technical and social resources of developing nations and relieve them of onerous international debt;

c) Ensure that all trade supports sustainable resource use, environmental protection and progressive labour standards; and

d) Require multinational corporations and international financial organisations to act transparently in the public good, and hold them accountable for the consequences of their activities.

### 11) Affirm gender equality and equity as

prerequisites to sustainable development and ensure universal access to education, health care and economic opportunity.

a) Secure the human rights of women and girls and end all violence against them;
b) Promote the active participation of women in all aspects of economic, political, civil, social and cultural life as full and equal partners, decision makers, leaders and beneficiaries; and
c) Strengthen families and ensure the safety and loving nurture of all family members.

12) **Uphold the right of all, without discrimination, to a natural and social environment supportive of human dignity, bodily health and spiritual well-being with special attention to the rights of indigenous peoples and minorities.**

a) Eliminate discrimination in all its forms such as that based on race, sexual orientation, religion, language and national, ethnic or social origin;
b) Affirm the right of indigenous peoples to their spiritual knowledge, lands and resources and to their related practice of sustainable livelihoods;
c) Honour and support the young people of our communities, enabling them to fulfil their essential role in creating sustainable societies; and
d) Protect and restore outstanding places of cultural and spiritual significance.

## IV.   DEMOCRACY, NONVIOLENCE AND PEACE

13) **Strengthen democratic institutions at all levels and provide transparency and accountability in governance, inclusive participation in decision making, and access to justice.**

a) Uphold the right of everyone to receive clear and timely information on environmental matters and all development plans and activities which are likely to affect them or in which they have an interest;

b) Support local, regional and global civil society and promote the meaningful participation of all interested individuals and organizations in decision making;

c) Protect the rights to freedom of opinion, expression, peaceful assembly, association and dissent;

d) Institute effective and efficient access to administrative and independent judicial procedures, including remedies and redress for environmental harm and the threat of such harm;

e) Eliminate corruption in all public and private institutions; and

f) Strengthen local communities enabling them to care for their environments, and assign environmental responsibilities to the levels of government where they can be carried out most effectively.

### 14) Integrate into formal education and life-long learning the knowledge, values and skills needed for a sustainable way of life.

a) Provide all, especially children and youth, with educational opportunities that empower them to contribute actively to sustainable development;

b) Promote the contribution of arts and humanities as well as the sciences in sustainability education;

c) Enhance the role of the mass media in raising awareness of ecological and social challenges; and

d) Recognise the importance of moral and spiritual education for sustainable living.

### 15) Treat all living beings with respect and consideration.

a) Prevent cruelty to animals kept in societies and protect them from suffering;

b) Protect wild animals from methods of hunting, trapping and fishing that cause extreme, prolonged or avoidable suffering; and

c) Avoid or eliminate to the full extent possible the taking or destruction of non-targeted species.

## 16. Promote a culture of tolerance, non-violence and peace

a) Encourage and support mutual understanding, solidarity and cooperation among all peoples and within and among nations;

b) Implement comprehensive strategies to prevent violent conflict and use of collaborative problem solving to manage and resolve environmental conflicts and other disputes;

c) Demilitarise national security systems to the level of a non-provocative defence posture, and convert military resources to peaceful purposes, including ecological restoration;

d) Eliminate nuclear, biological and toxic weapons and other weapons of mass destruction;

e) Ensure that the use of orbital and outer space supports environmental protection and peace; and

f) Recognise that peace is the wholeness created by the right relations with oneself, other persons, other cultures, other life, earth, and the larger whole of which all are part.

## Sustainable Development Goals (SDGs)

The SDGs were a follow up to the Rio Declaration, Millennium Development Goals and the Charter of the United Nations (The Earth Charter). The Rio+20 reaffirmed the commitment to fully implement the Rio Declaration, Agenda 21, the Plan of Implementation of the World Summit on Sustainable Development and the Johannesburg Declaration on Sustainable Development. The Rio+20 outcome document contained in *The Future we Want* mandated an open working group to develop a set of sustainable development goals for consideration and needed action by the General Assembly of the United Nations at its 68th session.

In the development of the SDGs, the OWG was closely guided by the purposes and principles of the Earth Charter. The importance of freedom, peace and security, respect for human rights, including the right to development and the right to an adequate standard of living, including the right to food and water, the rule of law, good governance, gender equality, women empowerment, and the overall commitment to just and democratic societies for development. In particular, the group reflected on the fact that the Planet Earth and its ecosystems are our home and that Mother Earth is a common expression throughout the world. In order to achieve a just balance among the economic, social, and environmental needs of the present and future generations, it is necessary to promote harmony with nature. It acknowledged the natural and cultural diversity of the world and recognised that all cultures and civilizations can contribute to sustainable development. One important observation was that every country was faced with specific constraints to achieve sustainable development and that developing countries needed additional resources for sustainable development.

The SDGs are as follows:

- Goal 1: End poverty in all its forms everywhere;
- Goal 2: End hunger, achieve food security and improved nutrition and promote sustainable agriculture;
- Goal 3: Ensure healthy lives and promote well-being for all at all ages;
- Goal 4: Ensure inclusive and equitable quality of education and promote lifelong learning opportunities for all;
- Goal 5: Achieve gender equality and empower all women and girls;
- Goal 6: Ensure availability and sustainable management of water and sanitation for all;
- Goal 7: Ensure access to affordable, reliable, sustainable and modern energy for all;
- Goal 8: Promote sustained, inclusive and sustainable economic growth, full and productive employment and decent work for all;
- Goal 9: Build resilient infrastructure, promote inclusive and sustainable industrialisation and foster innovation;
- Goal 10: Reduce inequality within and among countries;
- Goal 11: Make cities and human settlements inclusive, safe, resilient, and sustainable;
- Goal 12: Ensure sustainable consumption and production patterns;
- Goal 13: Take urgent action to combat climate change and its impacts;
- Goal 14: Conserve and sustainably use the oceans, seas and marine resources for sustainable development;
- Goal 15: Protect, restore and promote sustainable use of terrestrial ecosystems, sustainably manage forests, combat desertification, and halt and reverse land degradation and halt biodiversity;
- Goal 16: Promote peaceful and inclusive societies for sustainable development, provide access to justice for all and build effective, accountable and inclusive institutions at all levels; and
- Goals 17: Strengthen the means of implementation and revitalise the global partnership for sustainable development.

The SDGs are accompanied by targets and will be further elaborated through indicators focused on measurable outcomes. They are action-oriented, global in nature and universally applicable. The goals and targets integrate economic, social, and environmental aspects and recognise their interlinkages in achieving sustainable development in all its dimensions. They take into account different national realities, capacities, and levels of development and respect national policies and priorities. They build on the foundation laid by the MDGs, seek to complete the unfinished business of the MDGs and respond to new challenges.

## Reconciliation

1) First, it is important to answer the question: ***What are the Earth Charter and the SDGs?*** In 2000, the ***Earth Charter*** was launched at The Hague, Netherlands. The Earth Charter is an inscriptive document that provides a declarative insight into the nature and scope of sustainable development and sustainability. In this endeavour it builds on the earlier work by the United Nations as elucidated in the documents such as *World Conservation Strategy* and *Caring for the Earth* and in several other outcomes of conferences and workshops. The Earth Charter is basically a civil call for sustainability and a declaration of fundamental principles for building a just, sustainable and peaceful society in the 21$^{st}$ century, based on respect for nature, diversity, universal human rights, economic justice and a culture of peace. The charter sets forth a concise formulation of the meaning of sustainable living and development. It is a living charter with the power to unite people for a common purpose: *care and concern for the whole community of life*. The participants in implementing the charter should include students, governments, leaders, local authorities, communities and international agencies.

   The SDGs, on the other hand, are strategic goals that single out priority areas laid bare by the Earth Charter that need to be implemented in order to achieve sustainable development.

2) Second, what do the Earth Charter and SDGs entail? The Earth Charter attempts to provide an insight into the nature and scope of sustainable development and sustainability with a view to making them clear to the global community. It singles out the four dimensions of sustainable development: Ecological, social, economic, and political dimensions. The Charter enumerates 16 principles based on a further four themes, namely: ***a) Respect and care for the community of life; b) Ecological integrity; c) Social and economic justice; and d) Democracy, nonviolence and peace***. These themes cut across the four dimensions of sustainable development. In turn, each of the four themes contains four principles, making a total of 16 principles. Each of the four principles for each theme is elaborated on through two or more explanatory statements which are conceptual rather than action-oriented. The 16 are therefore interdependent principles for a

*sustainable way of life* as a common standard, by which the conduct of all individuals, organisations, businesses, governments, and transnational institutions is to be guided and assessed.

On the other hand, 17 SDGs are goals designed to enhance sustainable development across global communities. Each goal is accompanied by targets which are further elaborated through indicators focused on measurable outcomes. The targets are aspirational, action-oriented, global in nature and universally applicable. The goals and targets integrate ecological, social, economic and political aspects and recognize their linkages in achieving sustainable development in all dimensions. The 17 are therefore related goals for *sustainable economic growth* as a common standard, by which the conduct of all individuals, organisations, businesses, governments, and transnational institutions is to be guided and assessed,

3) Third, what strategies are put in place to implement and monitor the success of the Earth Charter and the SDGs? The key strategy adopted by the Earth Charter is the raising of awareness among the global community focusing on individuals, students, government leaders, local organizations and communities, local authorities, businesses and international agencies through various communication channels. In this way, the Earth Charter aims at creating a shared vision of basic values to provide an ethical foundation for the emerging world community and help build a sustainable world based on respect for nature, diversity, universal human rights, economic justice and a culture of peace. It is basically a civil call for sustainability and a declaration of fundamental principles for building a just, sustainable and peaceful society in the 21$^{st}$ century, based on respect for nature, diversity, universal human rights, economic justice and a culture of peace. The charter sets forth a concise formulation of the meaning of sustainable living and development. It is a living charter with the power to unite people for a common purpose: *care and concern for the whole community of life.*

The SDGs are to be implemented by each country and the role of national policies, domestic resources and development strategies will be important in the implementation process. Since this process is expensive developing countries need additional resources for sustainable development and financial strategies will have to be put in place. Thus implementation of the SDGs will depend on global partnership for sustainable development with the active engagement of governments, civil society, the private sector, and the United Nations system.

4) Fourth, the Earth Charter is the product of a decade long worldwide, cross-cultural, civil society dialogue on common goals and shared values, offering an inclusive understanding of sustainable development (UNESCO, 2006). Its key features are:

a) It provides an excellent example of an inclusive vision of the fundamental principles for building a just, sustainable, and peaceful world;

b) Its principles build upon international, environmental conservation, and sustainable development law and the various UN meetings that took place in the 1990s. It endeavours to consolidate and extend a number of international law principles reflecting the emerging consensus in global civil society;

c) It was endorsed by the 2003 UNESCO General Conference as an important ethical framework for sustainable development and a valuable teaching tool; and

d) It sets forth a concise formulation of the meaning of sustainable living and development.

The SDGs, on the other hand, are strategic goals that single out priority areas laid bare by the Earth Charter that need to be implemented in order to achieve sustainable development. The SDGs originated from the Rio+20 outcome document contained in *The Future we Want which* mandated an open working group(OWG) to develop a set of sustainable development goals for consideration. The goals were endorsed by the General Assembly of the United Nations at its 68th session.

The fundamental similarities and differences are explicit in Table 12.1

**Table 12.1: Differences between Contents of Earth Charter and SDGs:**

| Sustainable development dimensions | Broad Earth Charter principle/theme | Earth Charter Principle | SDG |
|---|---|---|---|
| Ecological dimension | -Respect and care for the community of life | 1a; 2; 15a, b, c; 16e | 6; 7; 13; 14; 15 |
| | -Ecological integrity | 2a, b;  5; 6; 7; 8 | |
| Social /Economic Dimension | Social and economic Justice | 3b; 4;  9; 10; 11; 12 | 1; 2; 3; 4; 5; 8; 9; 11; 12 |

| Political dimension | Democracy, nonviolence, and peace | 3a; 13; 14;16 | 1f; 2; 10; 16a-d; 17 |

## Summary

In this chapter, it became apparent that the development model that has hitherto encouraged wasteful patterns of production and consumption has caused unprecedented environmental destruction, depletion of resources and extinction of species. In addition, vices such as a steep rise in population, inequitable distribution of resources, injustice, poverty, ignorance, and violent conflict are widespread and the cause of ecological, social, economic and political instability. The fabric of global security is threatened. The need for the creation of sustainable communities is now more compelling than ever before. In order to build a sustainable global community, the nations of the world must fully abide by the international agreements and support the implementation of major guidelines and principles for sustainable living such as those espoused in the Earth Charter and Sustainable Development Goals (SDGs).

This chapter has provided a critical analysis of the fundamental principles and goals for sustainable living contained in the Earth Charter and SDGs.

## End of Chapter Activities

Explain the differences and similarities between the Earth Charter and the SDGs. Why are the two critical in guiding sustainable development and sustainability activities?

## BIBLIOGRAPHY

The Earth Charter www.EarthCharter.org

UNESCO (2006)
    United Nations Decade of Education for Sustainable (UNDESD)
    Development: Framework for the UNDESD International
    Implementation Scheme. Paris: UNESCO

# 13

## CHAPTER 13

## ENVIRONMENTAL CONSERVATION AND MANAGEMENT

### Introduction

In the previous chapter, you were introduced to the concept of sustainable development and sustainability. In this chapter, will learn about the various ways in which Kenyan societies may conserve and manage their environments for the purpose of preserving the stability of ecosystems and attaining sustainability.

**Expected Learning Outcomes**

By the end of this topic you should be able to:

- Demonstrate an understanding of development, environmental conservation and environmental management;
- Demonstrate the ability to use the instruments of environmental management in Kenya;
- Discuss the techniques of environmental management in Kenya; and
- Analyse critically the initiatives for the attainment of sustainable development in Kenya.

## Need for Environmental Conservation and Management

Our relationship with the biosphere will continue to deteriorate until a new order is achieved, a new environmental ethic adopted, our populations stabilize, and sustainable development becomes the rule rather than the exception. Among the pre-requisites for sustainable development is the **conservation and management of environmental resources**. However, before we examine the tools and techniques used in environmental conservation and management, we shall first define the two terms.

### Environmental Conservation

This is defined as the management of human use of the biosphere so that it may yield the greatest sustainable benefit to present generations while maintaining its potential to meet the needs and aspirations of future generations. Thus conservation is positive, embracing *preservation, maintenance, sustainable utilisation, restoration and enhancement* of the natural environment, including the living resources (plants, animals and micro-organisms and the non-living elements on which they depend). Conservation ensures that utilisation of environmental resources is sustainable and the ecological processes and genetic diversity essential for the maintenance of the resources are safeguarded.

### Environmental Management

This is a decision-making process in terms of planning, identifying tools, organising, directing, allocating resources and recognising and developing ways and strategies of using environmental resources in such a way that their supply will be balanced over time and their quality assured for future generations. Its overall purpose is to achieve environmental quality and better living standards of the people (i.e. sustainable ecological, social, political, and economic aspects of the environment). Environmental management is, therefore, *a systematic and orderly allocation and utilisation of environmental resources including land, buildings, water, soil and forests in order to achieve optimum economy, convenience and aesthetics and consequently sound environmental management*.

Note that planning is key to the process of environmental management which in turn facilitates the implementation of the plans. Environmental planning is the first function of environmental management, on which other functions, such as identifying tools, organising, directing and controlling parameters depend. It involves data gathering and analysis so that alternatives can be identified and evaluated in the decision-making process. This process forecasts what is needed for the future, setting objectives for the designed results, and developing strategies for how to achieve the goals. Priorities must be set and the strategies need to be sequenced in a time frame to accomplish the goals. Policies and procedures are developed. Budgets are used as planning and controlling tools to allocate resources.

Environmental planning is essential if optimum use is to be made of available resources and if sustainability is to be achieved. It is based on research, without which wrong choices may be made that impair sustainability sometimes permanently. Lack of planning in Kenya is leading to unbalanced development thereby forming uneconomical agglomerations, ecologically degraded areas and overexploited resources, especially in rural areas. In urban areas, we lack integrated environmental planning that focuses on development at the expense of ecological, social, economic and political considerations altogether. There is, therefore, need for assessment of the environment in terms of not only the economic aspects but also environmental aspects to achieve ecological balance and sustainability. There is a need to use environmental planning as a tool for environmental protection and the priority actions needed to be taken.

## Development

Development is the modification of the biosphere and the application of human, financial, living and non-living resources to modify the biosphere in order to produce goods and services needed to satisfy human needs and wants and to improve the quality of human life. However, the development process must take account of social, economic, political and ecological factors of the living and non-living resources-base, i.e. it must be sustainable.

Thus while development aims to achieve human goals largely through the use of biosphere, conservation aims at ensuring that such use can continue. *Environmental management is, therefore, integration of conservation and development to ensure that modifications to the planet Earth do not threaten the well-being of humankind, other forms of life and the planet itself. The development accruing from this process is sustainable development.*

## Instruments of Environmental Management in Kenya

As with all management functions, effective management instruments, standards and systems are required for environmental management. Instruments of environmental management are the tools or structures or infrastructure necessary for the implementation of anticipatory environmental policies, particularly in an effort to attain sustainability. The instruments presently used in Kenya include:

- Environmental legislation, regulations, policies and standards;
- Environmental Management Systems (EMS);
- Environmental Information Management Systems (EIMS);
- Environmental Impact Assessment (EIA); and
- Environmental Audit (EA).

### Environmental Legislation, Policies, Regulations and Standards

To achieve the objectives of environmental management we need proper environmental governance structures. Environmental governance entails the formulation of comprehensive environmental policies and the enactment of supportive legislative regimes in the form of laws, standards, and regulations as well as strong institutions to control activities that may damage the quality of the environment.

### Environmental Law

**Laws** are rules established by authority, society or custom to guide harmonious existence of humankind. The rules are established through legislation (Statutes), judicial decisions (case laws) custom (common law) or administrative decisions (administrative law).

*Government laws* are established by parliament (legislative body), while **Statute Law** consists of formal documents or decrees enacted by parliament declaring, commanding or prohibiting something. Environmental Management and Coordination Act no. 8 of 1999 is an example of legislation that has revolutionalised the management of the environment in Kenya.

***Administrative Law*** arises from executive orders, administrative rules and regulations and enforcement decisions in which statutes passed by the legislature are interpreted in specific applications and individual cases.

***Environmental Law*** constitutes a special body of official rules, decisions and actions concerning environmental quality, natural resources and ecological sustainability. Policies must be enacted into law to be effective. Hence sound environmental management requires effective legislation. However, the development of environmental laws in Kenya has been until recently piecemeal and haphazard. This has been characterised by:

- Gaps, duplication, conflicts in various laws;
- Lack of coordination among agencies responsible for conservation across the sectors such as agriculture, forestry, fisheries, water, wildlife, rural development, etc;
- Lack of skilled personnel due to inadequate training, infrastructure, salaries, etc; and
- Poor administration organisation.

For the above problems to be remedied we need enforcement of environmental laws, this is best done by an agency empowered by law. We also need to conduct regular environmental appraisals and assessments as well as monitoring to gauge the effectiveness of the law.

## International Treaties and Conventions

Although many international treaties and conventions have been passed to protect the global environment, most are vague or toothless. Some innovative measures have been devised to compel compliance. Some alternatives to adversarial litigation include:

- Arbitration;
- Mediation; and
- Community-based planning.

Examples of International treaties/conventions:

- Convention on International Trade in Endangered Species (CITES). This was not enforced until 14 years after its ratification in 1973;

- Convention on Biological Diversity – was enforced just after one year when it was ratified (1992);
- Montreal protocol (1987) to limit the use of CFCs in industries by 50%;
- Vienna Convention (1985) on CFCs production; and
- Kyoto protocol (See SOE, 2003, pages 126 – 127).

## Environmental Policies

*Policy* is a plan or statement of intention, either written or stated, about a course of action or inaction intended to accomplish some end. *Public policy* refers to the principles, laws, executive orders, codes or goals established by a governmental body or institution intended to accomplish some end in the public interest. *The environmental policy then refers to official rules and regulations concerning the environment that are adopted, implemented and enforced by some government agency as well as general public opinion about environmental issues.* The best environmental policies are those which incorporate economic, ecological, social and political considerations in the development process as a way of enhancing sustainability. Such policies involve actions to ensure that conservation and other environmental requirements are taken fully into account early in development projects.

Kenya has key environmental policy responses to the following thematic issues: poverty, climate variability, air pollution, land degradation, habitat loss, species loss, water resource use, water quality, urban conditions, and deforestation contained in the **National Environment Policy** of 2013.

## Environmental Regulations and Standards

The development and gazettement of Environmental Standards and Regulations has been done by NEMA. The following are now available and in operation:

- Environmental (Impact Assessment and Audit) Regulations, 2003;
- Water Quality Regulations, 2006;
- Conservation of biological resources, access and benefit sharing 2006;
- Fossil Fuels Regulations, 2006;
- Controlled Substances (Ozone Layer Depleting Substances) Regulations, 2007; and
- Regulations and standards being drafted include Air Quality, Noise

Pollution, Chemical and Toxic Substances, Wetlands, Lakeshores and River Banks, and Economic Instruments.

This is the process of using specialised devices to find out exactly what is going on with regard to the various environmental factors. The information is then disseminated to foster the integration of development and conservation.

We need to have an environmental monitoring system to gather the necessary data and information about our national environment. At present, UNEP has established an international monitoring programme called **Earth Watch** to monitor and disseminate information about the **State of the Earth**. The programme has two components:

- **Global Environmental Monitoring System (GEMS)** – This gathers information on the quality of air, food and water resources. It is located in Nairobi; and
- **INFOTERRA – International Environment Information Network** – Which deals with information acquired by GEMS for the purpose of dissemination.

We need to establish our national environmental monitoring system which could benefit from the success of Earth watch. Some of the things that should be monitored constantly include:

- The extent of vegetation cover;
- Level of water systems;
- Tectonic movements;
- Climate change;
- The extent of marginal lands;
- Land use patterns and changes;
- Food production; and
- Environmental health and safety.

Environmental monitoring is essential for:

- Ensuring that environmental impacts don't exceed the legal standards;
- Checking the implementation of mitigation measures, especially in projects undertaking EIA; and

- Providing early warning of potential environmental damages.

The following principles underlie environmental monitoring:

- Determine the indicators to be used in monitoring activities;
- Collection of meaningful and relevant data;
- Application of measurable criteria in relation to chosen indicators;
- Reviewing objective judgments on the data collected;
- Draw tangible conclusions based on the processing of information;
- Making rational decisions based on the conclusion drawn; and
- Recommendation for improved mitigation measures to be undertaken.

## Legal Provision for Environmental Management in Kenya

The Environmental Management and Coordination Act (EMCA) of 1999 provides the appropriate legal and institutional framework for the management of the environment in Kenya. It is umbrella legislation that provides guidance, coordination and harmonization of all environmental laws in the country. The 77 statutes relating to the management and conservation of the environment were hitherto sector specific. Some of these have inadequate provisions that don't address environmental issues such as prosecuting offenders, while others contain penalties that are not commensurate with the offences and thus offer insufficient punitive measures to deter offenders.

The first provision regarding environmental management was the establishment of the umbrella body under which the management of the environment must operate. The EMCA (1999) led to the establishment of the National Environmental Management Authority (NEMA) as a coordinating and law enforcement agency. This is set in section 9 (1) of EMCA which states:

> *"The object and purpose for which the Authority is established is to exercise general supervision and coordination over all matters relating to the environment and to be the principle instrument of Government in the implementation of all policies relating to the environment"*

Section 9 (2) then details 17 statutory functions that NEMA shall undertake including:

- Coordination of various environmental management activities being undertaken by the lead agencies and promoting the integration of environmental considerations into development policies, plans, programmes and projects with a view to ensuring proper management;

- Rational utilisation of environmental resources on sustainable yield basis for the improvement of the quality of human life;
- Taking stock of natural resources in Kenya and their utilisation and conservation;
- Carrying out surveys that may assist in proper conservation and management of the environment;
- Advising the Government on legislative and other measures for the management of the environment or the implementation of relevant international conventions, treaties and agreements relating to the environment;
- Mobilising and monitoring the use of finances and human resources for environmental management; and
- Preparing and issuing an annual report on the state of the environment in Kenya and in this regard directing any lead agency to prepare and submit to it a report on the state of the sector of the environment under the administration of that lead agency.

Secondly, EMCA made provisions on the management of different significant environments. EMCA(1999) Part v, section 42 – 57, provides guidelines on the activities that should not be conducted on a wide range of environments, such as rivers, lakes, wetlands, lakeshores, coastal zones and river banks. It also provides orders and suggests the need for provisions of regulations and standards to ensure proper management of these environments.

Thirdly, EMCA (1999) created several statutory organs for coordinating and directing environmental management activities. These include:

- National Environment Council (NEC);
- National Environmental Management Authority (NEMA);
- National Environment Tribunal (NET);
- Public Complaints Committee (PCC);
- National Environmental Action Plan committee (NEAPC);
- National Environment Trust Fund (NETF);
- Standards and Enforcement Review Committee (SERC);
- Technical Advisory Committee (TAC) on Environmental Impact Assessments (EIAS) and Environmental Audits (EAs);
- Provincial Environmental Committees (PECS); and

- District Environmental Committees (DECS).

Fourthly, EMCA (1999) also provides for the decentralisation of environmental management from central to lower levels of government. This includes the involvement of communities in the planning and management of environmental resources as follows:

- PECS and DECS facilitate the implementation of environmental policies and sectoral action plans at lower levels;
- The coordinating and supervisory role of NEMA provides for consultation with lead agencies and thereby integrates environmental concerns in all policies, programmes, plans and projects; and
- Partnerships between government and the private and non-governmental sectors promote a healthy and clean environment at all levels.

Fifthly, the Act takes into consideration the significance of environmental planning in environmental management. The operationalization of EMCA No. 8 of 1999 provides for the formulation of environmental action plans in which the principle of sustainable development through incorporation of participatory dimension provides for the inculcation of social responsibility. For example, Environmental Development Plans (EDP) through Participatory Environmental Planning (PEP) is being embraced by the Physical Planning Department through its Strategic Environmental Assessment (SEA). In addition, Part IV, section 37(1) of EMCA (1999) establishes the National Environmental Action Plan (NEAP). The NEAP committee is responsible for national economic planning and development. It prioritises environmental activities for the country for implementation across sectors for every five years. The NEAP contains information drawn from the District Environmental Action Plans (DEAPS) and Provincial Environmental Action Plans (PEAPS).

This development is important because environmental planning in Kenya has for many years been limited to physical planning by the Physical Planning Development provided in the Physical Planning Act (Cap 286) and the Local Government Act (Cap 265). The focus was on providing a well-balanced human settlement with habitable environments. However, this process has not kept pace with sustainable development requirements, resulting in unsustainable human settlements both in rural and urban areas. We can observe overcrowding, inadequate access to safe water, sanitation and proper drainage, encroachment on sensitive environments such as wetlands, water catchments and biodiversity habitats as some of the features characterising unsustainability.

Sixthly, the National Environment Management Authority (NEMA) is mandated under EMCA No. 8 of 1999, and as provided for in the Environmental (Impact Assessment and Audit) Regulations 2003, to cause organizations and project developers to undertake Environmental Impact Assessment (EIA). According to section 58 of EMCA No. 8 of 1999, all new enterprises and projects must undergo an Environmental Impact Assessment (EIA).

The projects to be subjected to EIA are specified in the second schedule of EMCA 1999 and include:

- Urban development;
- Transportation;
- Dams, rivers and water resources;
- Aerial spraying;
- Mining, including quarrying;
- Forestry related activities;
- Processing and manufacturing;
- Electrical infrastructure;
- Waste disposal;
- Natural conservation areas, nuclear reactors, biotechnology; and
- Any other that may change the environment.

Seventhly, NEMA is mandated under EMCA No. 8 of 1999 and as stipulated in second schedule of the Act and in the Environmental (Impact Assessment and Audit) Regulations (2003) to conduct the Environmental Audit (EA) of ongoing projects and/or have been in operation prior to the regulations or new projects undertaken after completion of an Environmental Impact Assessment study report and a license issued. The goal of Environmental Audit is to establish if proponents of projects are complying with environmental requirements and enforcing legislation.

An environmental auditor appraises all project activities, including the production of goods and services, taking into account environmental regulatory frameworks, environmental standards, environmental health and safety measures and sustainable use of natural resources.

## Summary

In this chapter, you have learned that our relationship with the biosphere will continue to deteriorate until a new order is achieved, a new environmental ethic adopted, our populations stabilise, and sustainable development becomes the rule rather than the exception. Among the prerequisites for sustainable development is the **conservation and management of environmental resources**. The tools and techniques used in environmental conservation and management were examined and the impact of EMCA was examined as was that of Environmental Impact Assessment.

## End of Chapter Activities

Examine the significance of using environmental management tools.

## BIBLIOGRAPHY

National Environment Management Authority (2004)
        State of Environment Report 2003, Kenya, Nairobi: NEMA
The Environmental and Coordination  Act, 1999
        Regulation 4(1) of Legal Notice NO. 101, the Environmental (Impact Assessment and Audit) Regulation 2003
The Environmental and Coordination (Amendment) Act, 2013

# 14

## CHAPTER 14

## ENVIRONMENTAL IMPACT ASSESSMENT (EIA) AND ENVIRONMENTAL AUDIT

Introduction

In this chapter, you will learn more about environmental impact assessment and environmental audit as two important ways of promoting environmental conservation and management for the purpose of preserving the stability of ecosystems and attaining sustainability. The two processes are supported by legislation, particularly the Environmental Management

214

and Coordination Act of 1999.

## The Concept of Environmental Impact Assessment (EIA)

### Definition of EIA

Environmental Impact Assessment (EIA) is a critical examination of the effects of a project on the quality of the environment. It is part of the project development process and is usually done at the initial stages of the project. It is a decision-making tool and should guide whether a project should be implemented, abandoned or modified prior to implementation. The process brings together a wide range of environmental, social and economic considerations before investments are committed to any development project. Any such project likely to have a significant environmental impact should undergo EIA.

### Objectives of EIA

The major goal of EIA is to ensure that decisions on development projects and activities are environmentally sustainable. The specific objectives of EIA are to:

- Identify the impacts of a project on the environment;
- Predict likely changes in the environment as a result of the development project;
- Evaluate the impacts of the various alternatives on the project;
- Propose mitigation measures for the significant negative impacts of the project on the environment;
- Generate baseline data for monitoring and evaluating impacts, including mitigation measures during the project cycle; and
- Highlight environmental issues with a view to guiding policy makers, planners, stakeholders and government agencies to make environmentally and economically sustainable decisions.

An EIA identifies both negative and positive effects of any development activity or project in terms of how it affects people, their property and the quality of the environment. It also identifies measures to mitigate the negative impacts, while enhancing the positive effects. It is thus used to predict and address the likely environmental consequences of a proposed development activity or project. The EIA is an important means of identifying and preventing problems and minimizing adverse impacts on the environment, thus reducing risks. EIA is, therefore, an essential step in environmental planning. If a proper EIA is conducted, then the quality of the environment can be effectively managed at all stages of a project-planning, design, construction, operation, monitoring and evaluation and decommissioning.

## Legal provisions of EIA

The National Environment Management Authority (NEMA) is mandated under EMCA No. 8 of 1999, and as provided for in the Environmental (Impact Assessment and Audit) Regulations 2003, to cause organizations and project developers to undertake EIA. According to section 58 of EMCA No. 8 of 1999, all new enterprises and projects must undergo an EIA. The Act further requires that any person being a proponent of a project, shall before financing, commencing, proceeding with, carrying out, executing or conducting or causing to be financed, commenced with, carried out, executing or conducting by another person any undertaking specified in the second schedule to EMCA, shall undertake or cause to be undertaken at his own expense, an EIA study and prepare a report for consideration by the Authority.

The EIA study report shall be submitted to the Authority in the prescribed form, giving the prescribed information and shall be accompanied by the prescribed fee. The Act also states that no licensing authority under any law in force in Kenya shall issue a trading, commercial or development permit or license for any project for which an EIA is required or for a project/activity likely to have a cumulative significant negative environmental impact unless the applicant produces an EIA license issued by NEMA.

In making a decision regarding an environmental impact assessment license, the Authority shall take into account:

- The validity of the EIA study report with emphasis on environmental, economic and social impacts of the project;
- The comments made by the lead agency and other interested parties;
- The report of a public hearing; and
- Other factors which the Authority may consider crucial in the implementation of the project.

The projects to be subjected to EIA are specified in the second schedule of EMCA 1999 and include:

- Urban development;
- Transportation;
- Dams, rivers and water resources;
- Aerial spraying;
- Mining, including quarrying;
- Forestry related activities;
- Processing and manufacturing;
- Electrical infrastructure;
- Waste disposal;
- Natural conservation areas, nuclear reactors, biotechnology; and
- Any other that may change the environment.

## Administration of Environmental Impact Assessment

The NEMA is mandated by EMCA no.8 of 1999 to administer the EIA. The project proponent pays for the entire EIA process. The fee payable to NEMA is 0.1% of the project cost. The EIA process is conducted by experts or firms registered by NEMA. The proponent shall also in consultation with NEMA seek the views of persons who may be affected by the project or activity through posters, newspapers and radio; hold at least three public meetings with the affected parties and communities. The public may participate by either submitting written or by making oral comments which are considered in reviewing the EIA study report.

**The Environmental Impact Assessment Process**

The components of the EIA process include the following:

- ***Proposal or Project Identification***: The proponent or developer prepares and submits a project brief to the National Environment Management Authority (NEMA) the legal requirements. The brief should contain information on the nature of the project, its aims and objectives, the source of funding and predicted cost, the proposed activities at all stages of the project, types and sources of materials to be used, products and by-products, target groups, socio-economic benefits and disadvantages to the affected community, location of the project, and any other relevant information. The information is needed in for the next activities of the assessment process.

- *Submission of Proposal to NEMA*: The proponent submits a complete proposal to NEMA for consideration. After receiving the project brief, NEMA considers and sends it to the lead agency to make their comments upon which a decision is made as to whether the project should be implemented or whether it should undergo the rest of the EIA study. If the project is unlikely to have an impact on the environment the developer is allowed to proceed with the project. If the project is likely to have significant environmental impacts, then the ensuing EIA process is recommended.

- *Screening:* This is the process by which actions considered to cause significant environmental consequences are selected for the purpose of applying the EIA procedure. It is the first stage of the EIA process. The project is examined to see the possible environmental impact it could have in the immediate environment. The process has two stages: Initial screening and environmental appraisal. The *initial screening* is used to quickly identify those projects that do and do not require an EIA. *An environmental appraisal* is a more detailed study for those projects that may likely have an impact on the environment.

    Screening determines whether or not a proposal requires an EIA and if so, what level of analysis is necessary. If both initial screening and environmental appraisal show there are potential causes for concern this stage goes into a deeper consideration of possible impacts and remedies that are determined in the next stages of EIA. The process brings clarity and certainty to the implementation of EIA, ensuring that it neither entails excessive review nor overlooks proposals that warrant examination.

    The screening process may have one of four outcomes: No further level of EIA is required; a full and comprehensive EIA is required; a more limited EIA is required (environmental appraisal), or further study is necessary to determine the level of EIA required (initial environment evaluation or examination).

- *Scoping:* This is the process of developing and selecting alternatives to a proposed action and identifying the issues to be considered in an EIA. The issues for decision making identified in screening that need to be examined in the EIA are determined. *The terms of reference (TOR) for the*

*EIA study are drawn on the basis of the issues.* With the involvement of the public and other stakeholders, acceptable terms of reference for the EIA can be developed thereby reducing the likelihood of a major controversy once an EIA report (EIS) has been prepared. Scoping is usually performed by a team which comprises a leader and multi-disciplinary based experts.

The purpose of scoping is therefore to: identify concerns and issues requiring consideration in an EIA; determine the extent of an approach to these issues; provide an opportunity for public involvement; enable NEMA to brief the study team on the alternatives and impacts to be considered at different depths of analysis; and facilitate an efficient EIA report preparation process. The major activities of scoping include: preparation of a preliminary or outline scope of the proposal indicating objectives and description of the proposal, policy context and environmental setting, data and information sources, alternatives to the proposal, concerns, issues and effects identified, provision for public involvement, timetable for scoping, EIA, and decision making; making the provisional scope available to the public; drawing a list of the range of issues and concerns and evaluating their relative importance and significance to derive a short list of the key issues; organizing the key issues into the impact categories to be studied; amending the outline scope to progressively incorporate the information from each stage; establishing the TOR for the EIA including information requirements, study guidelines, methodology and protocols for revising work; and monitoring progress against the TOR, making adjustments as needed and provide feedback to stakeholders and the public.

The outcome of scoping should be a *project specification* or *terms of reference* for the EIA, which: describes the project proposals and regulatory controls; identifies the potential effects upon the nature and character of the site and its surroundings; specifies the baseline and prediction studies required ,including particular features of the environment which must be addressed such as a known sensitive habitat.; specifies any criteria which should form the basis of the evaluation of significance; identifies the parties to be consulted.

- ***Baseline Study:*** This is the collection of background information on the biophysical, social, and economic settings of the proposed project area and submitting the report to NEMA. Normally, information is obtained from secondary sources if a facility of the database exists or from research in the field.

- Biophysical information include: Flora and fauna and biodiversity indices (species richness, density, and distribution); rare, endangered and keystone species, endemic species; ecosystems-wetlands, mangroves, marshes, floodplains; effects on the ecosystems e.g. hunting, heavy metals etc.; soil-based-geology, topography, soils, seismology; atmosphere based-climate, meteorology, air quality, noise; water based-surf ace and groundwater hydrology and quality; ocean based-coastal and marine parameters, currents, bathymetry, sedimentation, and erosion.
- Socio-economic information: Demographic-population changes, health, income, skills, education; employment, infrastructure, cultural/historical resources; land uses-commercial, agriculture, parks, reserves, protected areas.

The information provides a description of the status and trends of environmental factors against which predicted changes can be compared and evaluated, as well as providing a means of detecting the actual change by monitoring once a project has been initiated. The information is usually presented at the start of the EIA report to NEMA.

- *Impact Analysis:* This is a detailed evaluation using a variety of approaches to determine the actual impacts of the project on the broad environmental dimensions, namely, physio-chemical, ecological, social, cultural, health, and economic impacts.
  - Physio-chemical impacts include: Those affecting soil and landforms such as causing soil erosion, floods, sedimentations; those relating to air, water, soil quality such as brick factory, or untreated discharge;
  - Ecological impacts: Those affecting vegetation, wildlife, crops, aquatic life, plant life forms, structure and function, interactions of flora and fauna to form ecosystems, impacts on Keystone, rare and endemic threatened species such as cheetahs;
  - Social impacts: Those affecting the socio-economic status of communities around projects and include: Demographic

impacts-displacement/relocation, population characteristics; institutional impacts-demand on government and social services, housing, schools, health, criminal justice, welfare; gender impacts-projects influencing the role of women, income generation, employment chances, and equity distribution; and

- Socio-cultural impacts: Quality of life-expectancy, doctors, schools, policeman per head; social organisation and structures-social networks, forum, CBOs; cultural life-rituals, language, and general lifestyle; dispute-resolution and processes, relation between generation and value systems; resource use-look out for distribution of residents from generation to generation (knowledge passed on over time),new residents (little knowledge on resources use and extract resources unsustainably), non-residents-just visit the area for exploitation, most dangerous group and cause most impact.

These factors are evaluated in quantitative terms and should include the working-out of potential mitigation measures. Some of the techniques used in this process include checklists, matrices, networks, overlays and Geographical Information systems, expert systems, and simulations.

- Checklists: Lists of features with explanatory guidance-general: on type of project; generic-on class of project/development; sectoral-particular project;
- Matrices: Diagrammatic representation that show cause and effect between proposed and the status quo, ticks and symbols to show impact type (direct, indirect, or cumulative), numbers to show scale, etc.;
- Networks: Show cause and effect of project and environment, depicts second-order (indirect) impacts;
- Overlays and GIS: Various themes are taken separately then aggregated into a composite representation of potential impacts, useful in rerouting linear development to avoid environmentally sensitive areas, good for landscape and habitat zoning at the regional scale; and
- Simulation: Mathematical models are developed which are used to analyse various parameters to simulate the future. The approach is data demanding.
- *Mitigation:* This involves invoking measures to avoid, reduce, or remedy predicted adverse effects of a project on the environment either in design, operational measures or relocation and where

appropriate to incorporate these into an environmental management plan or system. It also enhances social and environmental benefits of a proposal. The three principals that drive mitigation are:

- *Avoidance* - this gives preference to avoid and prevent adverse impact and advocates for alternative sites or technology to eliminate impacts;
- *Minimisation* - action taken during impact analysis to reduce degree, extent, magnitude or duration of adverse effects by scaling down, redesigning components of the project or taking supplementary measures to manage impacts; and
- *Compensation* - applied to remedy unavoidable adverse effects through rehabilitation of sites, restoration of sites to its original or better state, replacement of same resource elsewhere, or monetary compensation, relocation/resettlement of affected people.

- **Preparation of Environmental Impact Statement (EIS):** This involves the documentation of the impacts of the proposed project on the environment, the significance of the effects, and the concerns of the interested public and the communities affected by the proposal. The EIS process has proven to be one of the most powerful tools in environmental management. It requires more open and environmentally sensitive planning in both the agencies themselves and in private corporations seeking to do business with the government. An EIS can bring to light adverse aspects of a project that might otherwise remain hidden. It can provide valuable information about a proposal to proponents who can't afford to do their own research.

Every EIS must contain the following elements:

- Purpose and need for the project;
- Alternatives to the proposed action – including taking no action;
- Statement of positive and negative environmental impacts of the proposed activities; and
- Relationship between short-term resources and long-term productivity, as well as the irreversible commitment of resources resulting from project implementation.

A successful EIA report is that which is:

- Actionable-a document that can be applied by the proponent to achieve environmentally sound planning and design.
- Decision-relevant-a document that organizes and presents the information necessary for project authorisation and if possible permitting and licensing.
- User-friendly-a document that communicates the technical issues to all parties in a clear and comprehensive manner.

- *Review and Public participation:* While public participation is recommended at every stage of the EIA process, the final public participation is crucial. The stakeholders include local people, project beneficiaries, voluntary organisations, NGOs, and the private sector. The purpose of public participation is to: inform stakeholders about the project and its likely effects; canvass their inputs, views and concerns; consider and incorporate their views in the EIA and in decision making; increase public confidence in the EIA process and thus create a sense of ownership of the project/proposal. The principles that make public participation successful are:

  - Fairness: Avoid bias towards any stakeholder;
  - Openness/Transparency: Ensure steps and activities are well understood;
  - Relevancy: Focus on issues that matter;
  - Responsiveness: To stakeholder's requirements and inputs;
  - Inclusiveness: Cover all stakeholders; and
  - Credibility: Build confidence, trust and sense of ownership.

- *Decision-making:* The decision as to whether the project should be implemented is reached by NEMA once the report is studied in detail. NEMA will either accept one of the project alternatives, request further study, establish the terms and conditions for its implementation, or reject the proposed action altogether and the decision is communicated to the proponent.

- *Appeals:* The proponent may appeal against the decision of NEMA in case the project is rejected. The appeal is directly made to the National Environmental Tribunal. If the tribunal upholds the decision earlier made by NEMA, the proponent may further appeal to the High Court. The decision of the high court is final.

- *Implementation:* For those proposals that are accepted in full or with conditions to fulfil, NEMA issues the licence authorizing the proponent to implement the project.

- *Monitoring and Auditing:* NEMA conducts periodic monitoring to ensure compliance with environmental standards in the process of implementing the project. At the same time, environmental audits are conducted to determine: the actual impact of the project on the environment; the accuracy of the predictions made by EIA; the effectiveness of the mitigation measures and enhancement of the measures; the functioning of monitoring mechanisms.

## Environmental Audit (EA)

Environmental Audit (EA) is the systematic documentation, periodic and objective evaluation of how activities and processes of an ongoing project conform to the approved environmental management plan of that specific project and sound environmental management practices. A comprehensive EA promotes a safe and healthy environment at all stages of project operations, as well as decommissioning.

### Purpose

The purpose of EA is to establish if proponents of projects are complying with environmental requirements and enforcing legislation.

### Legal Provisions

NEMA is mandated under EMCA No. 8 of 1999 and as stipulated in second schedule of the Act and in the Environmental (Impact Assessment and Audit) Regulations, 2003, to conduct the Audit of ongoing projects and/or have been in operation prior to the regulations or new projects undertaken after completion of an EIA study report and a license issued.
An environmental auditor appraises all project activities, including the production of goods and services, taking into account environmental regulatory frameworks, environmental standards, environmental health and safety measures and sustainable use of natural resources.

## Summary

In this chapter, you have learned more about environmental impact assessment and environmental audit as two important ways of promoting environmental conservation and management for the purpose of preserving the stability of ecosystems and attaining sustainability. The two processes are supported by legislation, particularly the Environmental Management and Coordination Act of 1999.

## End of Chapter Activities

Examine the significance of EIA and EA in environmental management and sustainability

## BIBLIOGRAPHY

Muigua, Kariuki (2012)
>  Environmental Impact Assessment in Kenya. Unpublished paper presented to the Institute of Development Studies Students on 4th December 2012

National Environment Management Authority (2004)
>  State of Environment Report 2003, Kenya, Nairobi: NEMA

The Environmental and Coordination Act, (1999)
>  Regulation 4(1) of Legal Notice NO. 101, the Environmental (Impact Assessment and Audit) Regulation 2003

The Environmental and Coordination (Amendment) Act, 2013

www.ingramcontent.com/pod-product-compliance
Lightning Source LLC
Chambersburg PA
CBHW030306290526
45785CB00001B/233